بسم الله الرحمن الرحيم

In the name of God, most Gracious, most Merciful

Madina
Book Centre
343 Normanton Road
Normanton, Derby DE23 6UU
Tel. (01332) 368002

بِسْمِ اللَّهِ الرَّحْمَنِ الرَّحِيمِ

AD-DUNYA

The Believer's Prison
The disbeliever's Paradise

Muhammad 'Abd ar-Rahman 'Iwad

Dar Al-Taqwa

© Dar Al Taqwa Ltd. 1997

ISBN 1 870582 80 2

Translation: Asadullah Yate

Editors: Abdalhaqq Bewley and Muhammad Isa Waley

Production: Bookwork, Norwich

Published by:
    Dar Al Taqwa Ltd.
    7A Melcombe Street
    Baker Street
    London NW1 6AE

Printed and Bound by- De-Luxe Printers,
London NW10 7NR.
website: http://www.de-luxe.com
email: naresh@aapi.co.uk

Table of Contents

In the name of Allah, All Merciful, Most Merciful

Foreword

Praise belongs to Allah alone; I bear witness that there is no god but Allah and I bear witness that Muhammad is His slave and His Messenger; may Allah bless and grant peace on our Master Muhammad and on his family and Companions and those who follow them with *ihsan* until the Day of Repayment.

Anyone who reads the Qur'an with reflection and careful examination will encounter many truths which will illuminate the self, purify the heart and connect man with his Creator. The Qur'an is a light and guidance making the path clear for those with illuminated insight. The prophetic *Sunna* has increased the clarity and distinction of this path, for it is a commentary on the Qur'an containing a great deal of explanation. The *Sunna,* which is the manifest expression of the state of prophethood, increases the clarity and lucidity of the truths and realities of the Qur'an. In this way the features of the first generations (after the establishment of Islam) and the source of Revelation are combined for the believer in the Qur'an and the *Sunna.* The believer can live according to this primal guidance and take the path of the Companions by means of these two things, or at least attempt to, under the protection of the revealed Message and the guidance of the noblest of creation, Muhammad, may the peace and blessings of Allah be upon him.

Among the realities revealed by the Qur'an and explained by the *Sunna* are the realities of the life of this world. I have for a long time pondered upon these illuminating realities and have tried, after striving to understand, to communicate what has been formulated in my heart and mind to my Muslim brothers, to remind them of these realities so that those of them for whom Allah wishes good remember them and may return to the correct path.

1

One of the things which urged me on to this was my becoming aware in this life of ours of the excessive greed people have for this world. Almost everyone is captivated by its beauty and desirous to find security and tranquillity in it, as if it were an abode of permanent residence; whereas in reality it is nothing but a passageway and bridge to the Next World – it is the abode to which Adam fell following his disobedience.

> *"We said, 'Descend from it, every one of you! Then when guidance comes to you from Me, all those who follow My guidance will feel no fear, will know no sorrow.'"*
>
> (2:37)

It is the abode of conflict.

> *"We said, 'Descend as one another's enemies. You shall have residence on the earth and enjoyment for a time.'"*
>
> (2:35)

The *Dunya* is a period of passage and the planting ground for the Next World. He says, may He be exalted:

> *"You will live in it and die in it and you will be brought forth from it."* (7:24)

Thus it is not the abode of permanence but rather the abode of testing, of decay, of fall and conflict. So how is it that we have forgotten its reality? How is it that we make permanent plans for a place we will not be residing in, that we collect and store up what will disappear? How is it that we prefer the transient to the permanent? We have forgotten that the Qur'an reproaches the people whom Allah, may He be exalted, destroyed when they held fast to the transient and abandoned the life of endless timelessness and as a result became tyrannical, violent and oppressive.

> *"Do you build a tower on every headland, just to amuse yourselves, and construct great fortresses, hoping to live*

*for ever, and when you seize, seize as tyrants do? So fear
Allah and obey me."* (26:128-132)

Consequently I thought it would be useful to remind myself of
the states of the *Dunya* and transmit this reminder to my brothers
who share my belief so that that perhaps Allah may spare us.

The word *Dunya* is derived from the Arabic for 'low' or
'abased'; and in Arabic the word for the revelation of the Quran is
expressed as 'sending-down'. The *Dunya* is play and amusement,
beauty and boasting, idle vanity. Moreover the *Sunna* has
explained the reality of what it is. Consider what has been related
in the story of the Night Journey and the *Mi'raj* ascent when the
Dunya appeared to the Prophet, may the peace and blessings of
Allah be upon him, as an grey-haired old woman, her beauty having all but disappeared, the reality of her being now manifest, her
life-expectancy short. Her early beauty had been an illusion. The
Prophet, may the peace and blessings of Allah be upon him, turned
away from her when she called him.

Consider too, my brother in Islam, the story of Qarun and what
ignominy and torment befell him when he was duped by the illuso-
ry beauty of this world through his tyranny. His short-sighted con-
tempories were likewise seduced by it, saying:

*"Oh! If only we had the same as Qarun has been
given!"* (28:79)

Consider also the story of the owner of the two gardens in the
Surat al-Kahf (The Cave) who entered his garden, wronging himself.

*"He said, 'I do not think that this will ever end. I do not
think the Hour will ever come. But if I should be sent back
to my Lord, I will definitely get something better in
return.'"* (18:35)

And what was the result? Destruction and torment befell him.

Consider also the story of the owners of the garden in *Surat al-Qalam* (The Pen) who swore that they would harvest in the morning but did not say the redeeming words, "If Allah wills". What was the result?

> *"So a visitation from your Lord came to it while they slept and in the morning it was like burnt land stripped bare."* (68:19-20)

So their efforts were in vain, their striving futile, after denying the rights of the destitute to some of the harvest. There are many more examples of such lessons and admonitions.

The essential thing is that the *Dunya* is not a real abode for the believer, rather it is a seedbed. It has been said that the *dunya* is like a market which is established and then closed down after some have made a profit and some have made a loss. So it is not a good idea for the believer to abandon something which concerns his life in the Next World for the sake of his *Dunya*, not a good idea for him to gather up something he is only going to leave behind and is in effect only storing up for others

Wealth is a two-edged sword. Whoever makes advances from his wealth now is in fact giving preference to his Hereafter so that he may regain what he has given in advance. Whoever delays spending his money is holding on to his *Dunya* as he hates separating himself from it. A believer sows in this *Dunya* of his so as to harvest an abundant reward in his Hereafter, but a disbeliever will find himself crying out when his time comes.

> *"My Lord, send me back again so that perhaps I may act rightly regarding the things I failed to do!"* (23:100)

His Lord comments:

> *"No indeed! It is just words he utters."* (23:100)

So he will remain in the Fire crying out in despair.

"Our Lord, remove us from it! Then if we revert again, we will definitely be wrongdoers." (23:108)

Once more a reply comes from his Lord, may He be exalted.

"Slink away into it and do not speak to Me." (23:109)

There are many *ayats* similar to these in the Qur'an. I have mentioned a few just as a reminder.

If one examines this present life of ours we find that it is full of enjoyment and distraction. The beauty of the life of this world is multifaceted. We cannot complain of hunger as the People of the *Suffa* complained at the time of the Messenger of Allah, may the peace and blessings of Allah be upon him. Some of them would bind a stone to his stomach for days. Indeed they would suffer bouts of swooning from the effect of extreme hunger – and this has been narrated from Abu Hurayra, may Allah be pleased with him. Indeed we cannot complain of the bitterness of deprivation as most of us have more than enough to suffice us.

Our complaint is that we never have enough. We want more and more wealth. We demand ever more comfort and desire ever greater luxury. Someone who has a house seeks a palace. Those who have modern equipment and luxury articles demand yet more. Those who own cars envy the better car of their neighbour. Employees are never happy, always looking to higher posts and greater income. The list is endless but let these few examples suffice. In short, one of the characteristics of Hell has appeared in us, and I seek refuge with Allah from this. This Hell which is an unquenchable, burning desire for the *dunya*, is always saying, *"Is there any more?"* (50:30).

I can say straight off that I know no one who is so stricken by poverty and so consumed by need that he is unable to fulfill the basic demands of life. What incapacitates people is the violent torrent of devastating consumer demands. I am citing *hadiths* and *ayats* to those in authority and those who reflect so as to protect them and us from negligence and forgetfulness. We must remain constantly aware of Allah's words, may He be exalted:

"When they forgot what they had been reminded of, We opened up for them the doors to everything until, when they were exulting in what they had been given, We suddenly seized them and at once they were in despair."

(6:45)

And I am citing these *hadiths* and *ayats* to the reader as a way of convincing him of the urgency of his plight and I hope that this will be of use to him. I am not speaking to him of my own thoughts and opinions but rather I am speaking with the tongue of the *Shari'a* and Revelation. My notes accompanying these *ayats* are simply by way of direction and instruction. The reader is free to make up his own mind regarding the commentary and interpretation of the texts I will present before him. I have concentrated on subjects which I have found to be of importance. Among them are the inner reality of the *Dunya*, the danger of becoming caught up in *Dunya*, the importance of being abstemious in this world, the danger of luxury and the limits of necessity and other subjects broached in the *hadiths* and which illuminate and clarify the Qur'anic *ayats*.

I ask Allah, the Sublime, the Vast, that He place this work in the balance of my good actions and the balance of good actions of those who read it.

Finally, if I have been successful, then this is by Allah and if not then it is because of my self; and Allah is the Much-Forgiving, Most Merciful.

And praise belongs to Allah, the Lord of the Worlds.

The author

Chapter One
The Muslims and the *Dunya*

At the onset of the call of Islam, the Prophet, may the peace and blessings of Allah be upon him, was in Makka, calling to Allah together with a very small group of mainly weak and dispossessed people. He made the utmost endeavours on their behalf but they were driven out by their people who declared the famous boycott by which the Muslims were confined to a narrow valley for three years, nobody having any transactions with them except during the Sacred Months.

Then Allah gave them permission to emigrate to Madina and their circumstances changed. They were victorious over their enemies, and the Messenger of Allah, may the peace and blessings of Allah be upon him, promised that Allah would have them win the treasures of Khusraw and Caesar but said that he feared the trial of prosperous times: a trial and test which seizes the heart and intellect and which lulls man to sleep and causes him to become dependent on its sweetness.

It is well-known that the *Dunya* is the prison of the believer – however luxurious his life in it may be – and it is the Paradise of the disbeliever – however little is his share of its beauty may be. A trusted friend once told me a story which I would like to repeat here in order to illustrate this theme.

Once a Jew passed by Imam ash-Shafi'i, may Allah be pleased with him, who was hurrying and struggling behind his donkey loaded with oil. The Jew's clothes were filthy and his whole manner was repulsive. When the Jew met the Imam who was reclining in the shade and dressed in immaculately clean clothes, he stopped and asked him: "How is it that people can say that the *Dunya* is the prison of the believer and the Paradise of the disbeliever?" (indicating the blessings surrounding the Imam and the striving and toil in which he found himself): it was as if he was insinuating that

7

those words were not true and that if they were true then ease should be for the Jew and toil and struggle should be for the Imam who could expect his blessings in the Hereafter.

The Imam replied: "Yes, it is true that the *Dunya* is a prison for the believer and Paradise for the disbeliever, for it is certain that the blessings I enjoy now in fact represent a prison in relation to what awaits me in the Next World. And if you realised what torment awaits you, then you would know that this lower world you now enjoy is in fact a paradise compared to that." Thus the *Dunya* really is the prison of the believer.

As we have seen, the Qur'an reproaches those who cling to the *Dunya* and say that it is the aim of all their hopes and their final goal. There is no harm in wealth as long as it is from a lawful source, and people are not harmed simply by enjoying the good things of life's provision; but they most certainly will be if they make this the aim of their life and forget their Hereafter.

As the believer is in the prison of the *Dunya*, Allah has made it an obligation upon him to struggle not to be overcome by it. *Jihad* is the means of deterring and restricting disbelievers, the means of curbing the injustice of oppressors so that injustice does not increase and circumstances are not constricted for the believers. If oppressors are left to their own devices and there is no *jihad*, they will humiliate believers and seduce them from their *deen*. Allah, may He be exalted, says:

> *"Fight them until idolatry is no more and the* deen *belongs to Allah alone. If they give up, there should be no enmity towards any but wrongdoers."* (2:192)

So although the believer does not live for this lower world he must not allow wrongdoers to control his actions or to organize his affairs, for that would only result in disaster and tremendous affliction. Believers are faced by perils from all sides and everyone wants to prey on the belief and trust they have. The relationship of the disbelievers to the believers is explained by Allah, may He be exalted:

"They would like you to reject as they have rejected so that you are all the same." (4:88)

As for the People of the Book, their state is even plainer since they are as eager, or even more so, to bring trial and misfortune to the believers.

"The Jews and the Christians will never be content with you until you follow their religion." (2:119)

Then there are the hypocrites. Hypocrisy is a disease which eats away at the body of the community quietly and silently:

"When they meet those who believe, they say, 'We believe.' But then when they draw aside with their shaytans, *they say, 'We are really with you. We were only mocking.'"* (2: 13)

And in another *ayat* describing these people we find:

"When they meet you, they say, 'We believe.' But when they go away they bite their fingers out of rage." (3:119)

In face of this army of enemies who are lying in wait for the believers the believer must arm himself in the most powerful way open to him so as to prevent his *deen* from being harmed.

"Arm yourselves against them with all the firepower and cavalry you can muster, to terrify the enemies of Allah and your enemies, and others besides them whom you do not know. Allah knows them." (8:61)

If the perils multiply and the enemy troops encircle the believers, then they have no option but to fight.

"Fight them until idolatry is no more and the deen *belongs to Allah alone."* (2:192)

9

The first Muslims clearly fulfilled the *Sunna* of *Jihad* and in doing so their *deen* was assured for them and their *Dunya*, the life in this world, was set right. But today I see that the Muslims have abandoned the *Sunna* of *Jihad* and have laid down their arms and have been stripped of their *deen*. They have been distracted by events from their *deen*. They have been upset and unbalanced by their attachment to the *Dunya*. They have become lazy in the *deen*. They have encouraged one another towards the *Dunya* and the obstacles to the *deen* have increased. As a consequence of this the whole matter of their life does not go right. Those who lose their deen or treat the matter of its teaching lightly will also inevitably suffer loss in the affairs in this world.

> *"...losing both this world and the Next. That is indeed sheer loss."* (22:11)

It is related from Abu Musa al-Ash'ari, may Allah be pleased with him, that the Messenger of Allah, may the peace and blessings of Allah be upon him, said: "Anyone who loves his life in this world will harm his *Akhira* (Next Life) and anyone who loves his Hereafter will bring harm to his *Dunya*. So prefer that which lasts to that which vanishes."[1]

In this age we live under the influence of certain specific values, principles and trends. Many of the natural laws have been abandoned in favour of fallible human alternatives and science holds sway in many matters. Man has learned how to build buildings dozens of storeys high and how to equip them with electric lifts. He has installed machines which can control temperature, making it fresh and cool in summer and warm and cosy in winter. He has mastered electricity which he uses to work the appliances he has made to make life in this world more comfortable and to provide him with everything he wants. All this has made the acquisition of the things of this world the main aim and purpose of most people's lives. In this atmosphere and under the influence of these values people can basically be divided into two camps: those who are capable of striving and fighting and struggling, who float

---

1. Related by Imam Ahmad from trusted narrators and reported by al-Mundhiri, vol. 4, p. 317

to the top and those who are incapable of it, who sink to the bottom and become destitute.

This causes internal friction and *jihad* is replaced by sterile conflict between the haves and have-nots in society. There may be those who call to *jihad* but all impetus and stimulus towards it disappear. All thought has been distracted from death, from *jihad* and working for the Hereafter, except in the case of a few rare people. Those whose lives have become full of ease and comfort demand yet more material goods and those who have been afflicted by dearth and destitution seek relief through an impotent struggle fuelled by resentment against those who have more than them. Everyone is held in sway by the influence of material goods and new inventions – they being perceived as the real source of the good life. Thus the West, the source of the aid and loans needed to acquire these things, represents luxury and stability and has become a sort of ideal to be aimed at in the minds of most people rather than the source of corruption it really is.

But where is the *jihad* against this powerful source of corruption which has done so much to erode the hold of Divine Guidance over people's lives and has all but destroyed Islam as a political reality? In the short term perspective, there is no longer anything to be done but for the Muslims to make *jihad*. It is now incumbent upon the Muslims to rise up in any way they can.

Some Muslims have unfortunately gone to the opposite extreme and declared that most Muslims should be treated as unbelievers and that war against them is obligatory, while others have said it is necessary to make *hijra* from the Muslim community and that the ship must be abandoned. These people are simply hiding out on the edge of Islam rather than taking it on fully. They are rebelling against the Muslim community, which is worse than not fighting the unbelievers.

But there is no doubt about the destructive effects on the Muslims of Western dominance and their admiration of what it represents. The Community is weakened first and foremost by consuming usury and making usurious transactions. It is weakened by the nakedness of women. It is weakened by gambling. It is weakened by alcoholic drinks which have become legal in many countries which officially have Islam as their *deen*. It is weakened by the acceptance of many things forbidden by Allah and His Messenger.

The Community has become lax regarding the obligation of *zakat* so that it is left up to individuals to decide whether they wish to pay or not and those who do not are left to their own devices. The Prophet, may the peace and blessings of Allah be upon him, used to collect it and appoint agents to collect it, and the first Caliph made war on those who refused to pay the *zakat* to him - even though, in other respects, they still remained within the pale of Islam. Those in authority continued to collect *zakat* and spend it on the allotted categories (mentioned in the Quran) until the time came when the *Dunya* overwhelmed them.

Then rulers turned their attention to taxes and no longer concerned themselves with *zakat*. When this happened people began to become lazy regarding the group prayer and other trends manifested and ideas flourished which were opposed to the *deen*. Soon people began to espouse heretical ideologies amounting to disbelief, such as communism and socialism and liberal democracy. Many manifestations arose as a result of this disastrously unhealthy situation.

What concerns us is that when someone focuses on the *dunya* in this way it enslaves him and distracts him from his *deen* and even then his affairs in this world are not fulfilled. What, then, is the solution? The solution can only be found in the person himself, in his own will. It entirely depends on whether he wants to be saved or not. If he does, there are various means of being saved, one of which, for instance, is knowing the true reality of the life of this world. A man of intellect does not evaluate it for more than it is worth and does not allow himself to become a prey to his desires or a prey to shaytan. But if people are content with the situation as it is nothing can be done.

Even if the door to *jihad* is an open one, the door to *jihad* of the self is always open and the Muslim must be aware of the true reality of this world, his position in it, and the limits within which he should keep in respect of it. These are limits which should be understood by every human being although Islam confers a distinction on its followers by making them clear in the plainest possible way, allowing them to realise the reality of their situation. Reflect on how the Qur'an has explained the relationship between the human being and the rest of existence.

"Allah is He who created the heavens and the earth and sends down water from the sky and by it brings forth fruits as provision for you. He has made the ships subservient to you to run upon the sea by His command, and He has subjected the rivers to you, and He has subjected the sun and the moon to you holding steady to their courses, and He has subjected the night and the day to you." (14:32-33)

"Do you not see that Allah has made everything in the heavens and the earth subservient to you?" (31:19)

"...and that He has made the sun and moon subservient, each running till a specified term, and that Allah is aware of everything you do?" (31:28)

These and many other *ayats* concentrate on this aspect of existence, confirming that the earth and all cosmic phenomena have been created in order to serve man. Allah, may He be exalted, says in *Surat al-Mulk* (The Kingdom):

"It is He who made the earth subservient to you, so walk its trails and eat of what He provides." (67:15)

Allah's use of the words *"He has made subservient to you"* explain the true position of the rest of creation with regard to man. Creation is at the service of man, is subjected to him. We continue to enjoy the heat of the sun and its energy every day. The earth continues to rotate. The winds do not cease blowing, sometimes strongly, sometimes gently. All these things play a vital role in our lives. The springs of creational gifts have never dried up since the Divine Command went out to the heavens and the earth making them subservient to us – when Allah said to them:

"'Come willingly or unwillingly.' They both said, 'We come willingly.' In two days He established them as seven heavens and revealed, in every heaven, its ordinance."
(41:10-11)

Just as the heavens and the earth have been made subservient to man, so too have the animals and the birds.

"And He created livestock. There is warmth for you in them, and various uses, and some of them you eat." (16:5)

So reflect, O brother in Islam, on man, the regent whom Allah has made master of the other creational realities which share existence with him. Reflect upon the spectacle of his original creation: Allah made and created Adam with His own Hand and breathed His Spirit into him. Reflect upon the same spectacle with the angels before their Lord bearing witness to the superiority of Adam because Allah had taught him all the names. Reflect too upon the honour accorded to man on this occasion when Allah ordered the angels to prostrate to him and when Iblis rebelled and refused to make the prostration and the Lord of Power banished him from His mercy. Reflect too upon another marvellous event, the spectacle of Allah's primal contract with the human species evoked in Allah's words, may He be blessed and exalted:

"When your Lord took out all their descendants from the loins of the children of Adam and made them testify against themselves: "Am I not your Lord?" They said, 'Yes indeed, we bear witness to it!'" (7:172)

Despite the splendour of this honour and its momentous implications, the accursed Iblis was able to seduce Adam into disobedience and so Adam ate from the forbidden tree, breaking his contract with Allah.

"We contracted with Adam before, but he forgot. We found in him no firm resolve." (20:115)

14

"Adam disobeyed his Lord and became misled. But afterwards his Lord choose him and turned to him and guided him." (20:118-119)

Adam descended to the earth where he, and by extension the whole human race, became subject to discord and had to seek a means of livelihood, there having been no need for this before.

"We said, 'Descend as one another's enemies! You shall have residence on the earth and enjoyment for a time.'"
(2:36)

Reflect too upon the words of Allah in *Surat at-Tin* (The Fig):

"We created man in the finest mould..." (95:4)

referring to the original exalted position bestowed upon the human creature, some aspects of which we have discussed above, which are immediately followed by a reference to man's state after Adam's descent from this atmosphere of light and plenitude:

"...then reduced him to the lowest of the low..." (95:5)

Man is thus transferred from the light of the higher life in Paradise to the obscurity of the lower life, the *dunya,* of this world – although the door of return to that higher world of light has not been closed to all mankind.

"...except for those who believe and do right actions."
(95:6)

The door of return is open to people who fulfil these conditions, but not to everyone. The return to Paradise is a journey of purification in which only the *mu'minun* – the believers – are successful.

However, when Adam descended to the earth, a portion of his regentship remained, in that Allah made everything in the heavens and the earth subservient to him. He subjected other creatures to him so that he might devote himself to fulfilling a most sublime goal, the purpose of his existence on earth. Allah Almighty says:

"I have not created jinn or man except to worship Me."
(51:56)

Man is, therefore, at the summit of all the creational realities which surround him – and this in an ascending order based on the purpose of each created thing: that is the mineral, vegetable and animal kingdoms and then mankind. The mineral world is subservient to the worlds above it: those of plants, animals and man. The plants make use of the mineral world, taking their nourishment from it, as do the animals and man, each according to its nature. The plant world is subservient to the animals and to mankind, in accordance with the nature of each. And in the same way we can see that the animals are subservient to man, as the Qur'an explains. When we come to man, however, we find that he is not subservient to anything in this world – only to Allah.

Each kingdom leads to something which is greater than it and it is inevitable that man too should look upwards towards something of greater value than himself which seeks his service. It is not logical that every created thing should aspire upwards towards what is above it and then that mankind should be divorced from this upward aspiration and aspire to what is lower than himself. No, in this upward aspiration lies the meaning of man's existence and goal. Without it this goal is missed and the meaning is lost. The Qur'an continually emphasises this by drawing the gaze of the believer to the heavens. Just as the earth brings forth its hidden, inconceivably vast stores of minerals into the light of day and the plants come forth from the earth and strive upwards towards the sky, so man must strive heavenwards to the place whence he came.

"Your provision is in heaven – and what you are promised. By the Lord of heaven and earth, it is most certainly the truth, just as you have speech." (51:22-23)

Man puts the seed into the earth but this act is in fact connected to the higher realm of realities. Man is in this world for the highest possible purpose, the worship of his Creator and Lord. Allah has facilitated the means to this by making him master of the rest of creation. Is it proper for a master to change into a slave? Indeed, would any man be content to make his own servant his master? That would clearly be an unacceptable reversal of roles. It would result in being content with what is mean and base. If this happens the inevitable consequence is that man reverts to being the lowest of the low – and we seek refuge with Allah from this.

Islam binds the believer to his Lord. It facilitates for him his affairs in the world in order that he may achieve the sublime aim and goal for which Allah has created him. And praise belongs to Allah, the Lord of the Worlds.

Chapter Two
Reflections on the *Dunya*

Why is it that the character of the *Dunya* is hidden from people and that its guile and seduction are so pleasing to them? Why are their eyes drawn inexorably towards its transient beauty and how is it that they bury their dead but forget their own inevitable end? Most people live as if they were heading towards some other destination, far removed from the grave.

The word *dunya* is derived from an Arabic root meaning 'low'. That which is low implies descent and descent in turn means abasement and insignificance. It may also be derived from another root meaning 'nearness' because of its proximity to man and the ease with which he surveys it and because of its subservience and lowliness with respect to man; or, alternatively, in allusion to the fact that man's lot in it is near at hand and life in it is short. What, one may ask, is the worth of man's life span of more or less sixty years in this world in comparison to the endless aeons of time with Allah? Here is one example of what Allah says about time in His sight:

> "A day with your Lord is the same as a thousand years in the way you count." (22:45)

A Divine 'day', then, is equivalent to a thousand years by our reckoning. This clearly indicates a completely different way of measuring time, a kind of timescale quite outside our normal terms of reference. On this basis a life-span of sixty years – or even a hundred and twenty – is truly negligible. Taking the statement at its face value the duration of this shortest unit of Divine time is thirty human generations. Yet despite this how much importance the length of our lives takes on in our eyes! The only really important measure of our lives is faith and awareness of our accountability for our actions in this life.

Let us shift our attention to the ant world. Have you ever looked at a colony of ants? One ant runs behind another and a third and a fourth ... a tenth, a hundredth. This constant movement begins to burrow out a house in a wall or under a tree or in an open space. At great speed the colony of ants digs out its home and excavates a mound of earth. This hill gets higher as the ants hollow out the earth. We do not realise the huge amount of ant energy required to do this. Finally the job is done and their home is completed.

They put grains of wheat and other foodstuffs in the storerooms they have constructed. How many grains are needed to fill the stores of its house? Perhaps fifty grains of wheat or thirty of maize or a corresponding number of other grains. Thousands of individual ants are contained within their dwelling which is spacious for the ants but from our perspective no more than a few handfuls of earth dug up by a child at play. Yet how marvellous is the village of the ants when one observes it closely! It is completely self-contained and functions as a harmonious whole with an extremely complex social hierarchy each part of which fulfills its function efficiently. How are our villages and towns in this world any superior to this? It might well be argued that in many respects they are considerably inferior.

How generous our Lord is to give us the example of the life of the ants and their like to teach us the reality of our own situation! But in spite of this we act arrogantly in the earth, allowing our fantasies to delude us and fill us with vanity. In the light of this example of the ants many things may be understood, one of which is that in the sight of Allah this world is not worth so much as a gnat's wing. Allah *ta'ala* says in *Surat az-Zukhruf* ('The Gold Ornaments'):

> *"Were it not for the fact that people might become one nation, We would have assigned roofs of silver to the houses of those who reject the All-Merciful, and stairways up which to climb and doors of silver to their houses, and couches on which to recline, and ornaments of gold. All of*

*that is merely the furnishings of the life of this world. But
the Next World with your Lord is for the godfearing."*
(43:33-34)

This shows that there is no value whatsoever in the things
which most people consider so desirable and makes it clear why
the Qur'an admonishes those who prefer the life of this world to
the next world, those who are content with the life of this world
and find security in it, those who are heedless of the *ayats* of
Allah. The *Dunya* without faith is not worth anything at all. And
after all what is the world, all its alluring pastimes and pleasures
for? Brought down to its bare essentials it is no more than a little
food to satisfy our hunger, a drink to satisfy our thirst, some
clothes to cover our nakedness and a roof over our head. The
believer desires no more of the *Dunya* than this, just as the meagre
provision of a rider on a journey is sufficient for him.

The Messenger spoke truly when he said: "Anyone who spends
the night assured in his mind, sound of body and having enough
provision for the day has obtained the whole of this world." Air
conditioning, cars, aeroplanes, flamboyant clothes made of costly
materials, gold rings, expensive carpets, large rugs and lavishly
appointed offices – all things are worthless, all of these are in reality worth less than what an ant accumulates in its hole in the
ground.

*"The life of this world is nothing but the enjoyment of
delusion."* (3:185)

✽✽✽✽✽

Sayings of 'Ali ibn Abi Talib, may Allah be pleased with him, about *Dunya*

We would like to mention in this connection some of the say-
ings attributed to Imam 'Ali concerning the *dunya* and its reality,

may Allah be pleased with him and may Allah ennoble his face. It is worthwhile to reflect upon some of these views of his and to benefit from them.

Illuminating aspects of the *Dunya*

"Surely the *Dunya* is the abode of truth for those who affirm its truth and the abode of well-being for those who understand it, the abode of wealth for those who take provision from it and the abode of instruction for those who draw lessons from it. It is the mosque of those who love Allah, the place of prayer of the angels of Allah, the place to which the Revelation came, the marketplace of the Friends of Allah where they acquire mercy and gain the Garden in profit. Who, then, would find fault with the world when you have been instructed to keep your distance from it and called to separate yourself from it?"

Here 'Ali describes the different natures and characters which make up this world. He gives examples of its trials and afflictions in order to make people ready for the greater test of the Hereafter. He also shows how some people possess a passion for the joys and happiness of this world in anticipation of the blessings of the Hereafter. Such people set off with health and vitality, forestalling any possible calamity with enthusiasm and awe, in fear and caution.

The men who find fault with the world are those who despair early in the morning, who do not draw lessons from the world, and who experience despair every time they lose something of it. Others, however, praise it because the *Dunya* reminds them of the Day of Reckoning. They act on this reminder and pay heed to it. The *Dunya* warns them and they respond to the warning.

Attachment to this world

"Anyone who awakes to the world in a state of sadness awakes to the decree of Allah in a state of anger."

"Anyone whose heart is attached to love of this world will be beset by three things: anxiety which will never leave him, greed for the world which will never depart from him, and a desire which he will never attain to."

The ephemeral life

"O people, you are beings over which fate and destiny are continuously vying with one another in this world. Each draught you drink could be the cause of your choking at any moment, as could each morsel of food. No one attains any of the blessings of this *Dunya* without relinquishing another of its blessings. No one constructs a building without destroying another in order to do so. Increase in food can only come after the exhaustion of previous provision. No inheritance can reach you except after the death of one of your relatives. The putting on of new clothes necessitates the taking off of old ones. The appearance of a new generation means the disappearance of the previous one."

The lessons of life

"Surely this *Dunya* which you have come to desire, which you seek after, with which you become angry or content, is not in fact your true home or the residence for which you have been created, nor is it that to which you have been called. It will not last for you and you will not last in it. Even if you have been beguiled by it, its evil has certainly given you prior warning. This world's guile and deceit are in fact averting you to its greed and rapacity in order to instill fear of it in you. So race each other towards the Abode to which you have been called. There is no harm in your missing out on anything in this *Dunya* of yours as long as you have got hold of the fundamentals of your *deen* just as there is no benefit in your getting hold of anything of the *Dunya* if you have missed out on your *deen*."

The rank and true nature of this world

" I would caution you against this world, for it is a transitory abode and not one of lasting substance. It is a world which has adorned itself by means of its deceit and guile and then deceives by means of its beauty. It is a world which has little significance in the sight of its Lord: a world in which the *halal* is mixed with the *haram*; a world in which good is mixed with evil, life with death, sweetness with bitterness. Allah, may He be exalted, does not make it attractive for His Friends and He is unstinting with it in the case of His enemies. The best people of this world are those that do without in the *dunya* and the worst are those who are rebellious. Things of the world which have been stored up will be used up and possessions of this world will be taken from their possessors.

"Those who have constructed buildings will see them fall into ruin. What, then, is the good of an abode which falls into ruin in the same way that any building does? What good is there in a life which is as ephemeral as provision itself, in a period of time which has no more durability than any journey? How is it that you are happy with the tiny amount of the *dunya* that you might obtain but are not saddened by the huge amount of the Hereafter which you will definitely lose? You become anxious about a tiny thing in the world which passes you by to the extent that it can be seen in your faces. You have as little patience with regard to that which slips from your grasp as if this were

the abode of permanent residence and as if your enjoyment of it would last for ever."

The states of this world and its wiles

" I warn you against this world, for although it is sweet
and green it is surrounded by desires. It endears itself to
people by the very fleeting nature of its existence and is
able to delight them with very insignificant things.
However, it causes all hopes to disappear and it adorns
itself with deceit. Its joys do not last and no security may
be found from its calamities and disasters. It is deceitful
and harmful, a barrier and obstruction which will
inevitably disintegrate. It is something which will exhaust
itself and perish. It both consumes and destroys. When it
does appear to fulfil the desires of the people who yearn
after it, it becomes as the likeness described by Allah: *'It
is like water that We send down from the sky and the
plants of the earth combine with it. But then it becomes
dry chaff scattered by the winds. Allah has complete
power over everything.'* (18: 44)

"Never does a man attached to this world rejoice without this being followed by his grieving. Never does he
enjoy the hidden aspect of anything during the good days
without the *Dunya* bringing him its manifest aspect during
the bad. He never has light rain fall on him in this world
from one cloud without the heavy rain of tribulation
falling on him from another. It is characteristic of the
Dunya that a man should begin the day in great acclaim
but end it enjoying total obscurity.

"If one side of the *Dunya* is deliciously sweet the other
is bitter and like the plague. No one will find pleasure in
its richness and abundance without also being exhausted
by its trials and tribulations. No one will go to sleep secure
in the evening without waking up to fearful events in the
morning. *Dunya* is a state of forgetfulness in which every-

24

thing contrives to deceive. It is a state of transience in which everything is in the process of annihilation. There is no good in any of its provision, except the provision of fear of Allah.

"How many who trust in the *Dunya* have been plunged into crisis by it, and how many who feel secure as to the *Dunya* have been struck down by it! How many a proud person has been brought low by it, and how many a haughty person humiliated! Those who live in it are constantly exposed to death and those who are healthy are constantly exposed to illness. Those who possess it will have it taken away from them and those who are powerful in it will inevitably be overwhelmed. Those of the world who are amply provided for will be struck by disaster and those who find safe haven in it will be made war upon."

Dunya and its deceit

"What can I say to describe an abode the first part of which is difficulty and the last part of which is annihilation? Even in that portion of it which is *halal* there is a reckoning and in that which is *haram* there is a punishment. Those who are rich are put to the test by it and those who are poor are in despair. Those who vie and struggle for its sake find that they fail to attain it and those who renounce it find it coming to them. Those who see through the *Dunya* will be given sight but those who look at it will be blinded."

The wisdom in rejecting the world

"O slaves of Allah, I advise you to reject this world, which in fact is abandoning you even if you do not wish to abandon it. It is a world which is wearing out your bodies even if you wish them to be rejuvenated. The likeness of yourselves and the world is that of travellers who are travelling

25

along a road. Some go the whole distance and arrive at their destination. They make for a mountain and reach it. Others, however, get held up and do not arrive at their destination.

"The excited seeker of this world is spurred on by it but he will inevitably be separated from it. So do not vie with each other for the power and glory of this world and do not be ensnared by its beauty and its good things. Nor should you be saddened by its difficult times and hardships, for surely its power and its glory are coming to an end and its beauty and its good things will soon vanish. Difficult times and hardships will inevitably come to an end and any period or space of time, however long, will run its course and every living thing will cease to be."

Chapter Three
The Reality and Truth of the *Dunya*

It is narrated that Abu Hurayra said: "I heard the Messenger of Allah say: 'Surely this lower world is cursed: everything in it is cursed except for remembrance of Allah, those who are steadfast in it, the man of knowledge and the one who seeks knowledge.'"[1]

We have begun this chapter with the above *hadith* in order to make the reader aware of the reality of the *Dunya*: such, then, is the reality of the *Dunya* and its status in the sight of Allah, may He be exalted. But how is one to escape this misfortune?

Remembrance of Allah is much mentioned by Allah *ta'ala* in the Quran. He says, for instance: *"So remember Me and I will remember you."* (2:152). It is by way of this remembrance that a person establishes that connection with his Lord which guarantees his salvation. It is by means of remembrance that the believer rises above the material things of this life, makes a connection with the Higher Assembly, purifies his self, refines his heart and gains victory over the opacity and grossness of this life and its material nature.

"Those who are steadfast in it" refers to those who are steadfast in their worship, in their right actions, in their acts of kindness towards people, in their maintenance of strong family connections, and in all those other actions which Allah has indicated He is pleased for his slave to perform, which He has laid down for them in the *Shari'a* and encouraged them to undertake.

"The man of knowledge" refers to people who have knowledge of matters of the *deen* and their requirements and knows about

---

1. Narrated by at-Tirmidhi who said that it is a good, yet isolated *hadith*; the curse is being driven from the mercy of Allah *ta'ala* and the *hadith* explains what are the gates of mercy.

what is permitted and what is forbidden. He is like a lighthouse guiding those who are confused. He is a model and support for those who act in the Way of Allah, reminding them if they forget and admonishing them if they become lazy or negligent. He establishes them firmly by his own certainty if they become embroiled in unfortunate situations.

"The one who seeks knowledge" refers to a person who is looking for the truth and who is capable of perceiving it in the darkness of ignorance and the grossness of the material world but who does not seek it for show or renown or desire rank and standing among people.

> It is narrated from Sahl ibn Sa'd that he said: "The Messenger of Allah, may the peace and blessings of Allah be upon him, observed: 'If the *Dunya* were worth a gnat's wing in the sight of Allah, He would not give an unbeliever even so much as a drink of water in it.'"[1]

We see the unbeliever enjoying the good things of this world, partaking of all of it and able to obtain all of its benefits. In spite of the fact that he is obstinate and rebellious in his rejection and attributes partners to Allah, Allah does not withhold anything from him but on the contrary extends his blessings to him – as Allah says, may He be exalted:

> *"Each one We sustain, the former and the latter, through the generous giving of your Lord; and the giving of your Lord is not restricted."* (17:20)

For the unbeliever, however, this divine giving is not a gift or a reward but rather an enticement and temptation. As Allah, may He be exalted, says:

> *"Say: As for those who are astray, let the All-Merciful prolong their term."* (19:75)

---

1. According to at-Tirmidhi says that this is a sound *hadith* although scarce in this transmission.

"We allow them more time only so that they increase in evil-doing." (3:178)

So the unbeliever may take whatever he is able to take of this world and that is the amount that has been decreed for him. In fact he is only grabbing hold of insubstantial matter and storing up worthless objects. If the *Dunya* were equal in worth to even the wing of a gnat in the eyes of Allah He would not have allowed the unbelievers to enjoy it while in their state of disbelief. In fact He is increasing their torment on the Day of Reckoning by establishing the evidence against them in this world.

> It is related from Ubayy ibn Ka'b that the the Messenger of Allah said, may the peace and blessings of Allah be upon him: "Surely the food of the son of Adam has been put forward as a likeness for the *Dunya*: however much one seasons it and puts salt on it one must not fail to see what eventually happens to it."[1]

The nature of the *Dunya*, then, resembles the food of man. In the first instance it appears deliciously inviting and stimulates him into wanting to eat, especially if it has been seasoned with peppers and spices. As soon as it is swallowed, however, it becomes transformed into something quite different and the body absorbs what it needs from it. Then what remains becomes excrement which is voided by the body. In this there is a clear admonition against falling into the temptations of the life of this world and being seduced by its deceptive beauty.

> It is narrated from Salman that he said that a group of people came to the Messenger of Allah, may the peace and blessings of Allah be upon him, and he asked them: "Do you eat food?" They replied: "Yes." Then he asked: "Do you take drink?" to which they replied: "Yes." He asked: "You absorb the best of it, do you not?" They again

---

1. However many spices and salt one adds to the food in order to make it even more delicious, in the end it will inevitably end up as faeces which man finds difficulty at even looking at, indeed is repulsed and disgusted by it.

replied: "Yes." Then he said: "And then you expel the rest, do you not?" to which they once more replied: "Yes." Then he said, "The final result of this food and drink is like the final result of the world. Each of you stands behind his house and holds his nose on account of the stench."[1]

Surely there is no more insignificant thing than the *Dunya*, nothing more despicable. It becomes decayed and rotten. How insignificant too are those who cling to it, and how despicable they are!

It is narrated from al-Mustawrad ibn Shaddad that he said: "I was among some riders who came to a halt with the Messenger of Allah, may the peace and blessings of Allah be upon him, before a dead sheep. The Messenger of Allah, may the peace and blessings of Allah be upon him said: 'Do you not see how despised a thing this was for the person who threw it away?' 'The fact that it was thrown away is certainly a sign of its being despised, Messenger of Allah!' He then said: 'The *Dunya* is even more despised by Allah than this is by its owner.'"[2]

This depicts a scene containing much instruction for us. The Messenger, may the peace and blessings of Allah be upon him comes to a halt in front of a dead sheep and points out to those with him how despised a thing it must be in the eyes of those who threw it away. His Companions could see that it was despised by the people who had owned it by the fact that they had thrown it away without any concern or regret for it. The perfection of humanity, may the peace and blesssings of Allah be upon him, then delivered a clear piece of wisdom to them, by drawing a parallel between the dead sheep and the *Dunya,* showing the attitude towards it that people of reflection and intellect should take.

---

1. According to al-Haythami, al-Tabarani has narrated this, and his narraters are men of soundness, without presumption, and it is a reliable *hadith*.

2. At-Tirmidhi describes it as a good *hadith*.

Jabir related said that he heard the Messenger of Allah, may the peace and blessings of Allah be upon him, say: "If the son of Adam had a valley full of date-palms he would want the same again and then the same again, desiring valley after valley. The belly of the son of Adam will never be satisfied until it is filled with earth."[1]

This *hadith* draws our attention to an ubiquitous characteristic possessed by human beings: the love of wealth, be it for palm trees or any other kind of property. The *hadith* ends by warning the believer not to let this characteristic of his get the better of him and not to let it distract him from his certain appointment with the Hereafter. The fact that "nothing will satisfy the belly of the son of Adam until it is filled with earth", apart from being an obvious allusion to the grave, is also an indication that everything which man desires will eventually become earth or is worth no more than earth, and that it is only the Hereafter that has good in it and is of lasting value.

According to Abu Hurayra, the Messenger of Allah, may the peace and blessings of Allah be upon him, remarked: "This world is a prison for the believer and a paradise for the unbeliever."[2]

Surely the believer suffers considerably in this world. He finds himself exposed to sudden desires which he must resist or violent wishes with which he comes into conflict. He is torn between permitted things which he strives after and forbidden things of which he is fearful. Within himself he has needs but it is to Allah that acts of obedience belong, so he must give priority to acts of obedience over his needs if they conflict with them. For this reason he fasts out of submission to the command of Allah and pays no attention to his feelings of hunger, in order to show to Allah his readiness to respond and obey. Likewise he gives away *sadaqa* and purifies his

---

1. This is narrated by Ahmad, Abu Ya'la and al-Bazzar and the men of these narrators are all sound.
2. According to at-Tirmidhi, this is a good and sound *hadith*.

wealth, by paying *zakat* despite his love of wealth, because his love for Allah, may He be exalted, is greater.

This world is a prison for the believer. He only moves towards desire within the limits imposed on him by faith and he does not aspire to any luxury without being held in check by fear of Allah and the wish to please Him. He knows that when his time comes he will find more with his Lord in the Hereafter than he could ever have imagined. As for the non-believer, he is not restrained by obedience to Allah nor does any divine command curb him, and so he is free from any restrictions in this world.

> 'Abdallah ibn 'Amr narrates that the Prophet, may the peace and blessings of Allah be upon him, declared: "This world is a prison for the believer and a *sunna* and when he leaves this world he leaves the prison and this *sunna*."[1]

> It is narrated from Ibn 'Abbas that 'Umar, may Allah be pleased with him, came upon the Messenger of Allah, may the peace and blessings of Allah be upon him, when he had been lying on a reed mat which had left its mark upon his side and he said: "O Prophet of Allah, if you were to take a mattress it would be softer than that." To which he replied: "What have I to do with the this world? There is no comparison between me and the *Dunya* but the likeness of the rider who travels on a very hot summer's day. He stops for shade beneath a tree for an hour during the day but then goes on and leaves it behind."

Surely human existence is a journey and the *Dunya* is nothing but a very short stage on a much greater journey. It is a place of transition in which the traveller stops to take shade, to rest a moment during the day. That is the reality of this life for a believer and for this reason we find the Prophet, may the peace and blessings of Allah be upon him, saying: "What have I to do with this world? It is not an abode of residence or a place of security."[1]

---

1. Ahmad relates this, as does at-Tabarani in a shorter version. The transmitters of Ahmad are sound except for 'Abdullah ibn Janada who is (only considered of the rank of being) trustworthy; the word *sunna* here refers not only to a pattern of behaviour but also to a regime of trial and hardship.

"The life of this world is only a game and a diversion. If you believe and are godfearing, He will pay you your wages and not ask you for your wealth. If He did ask you for it and put you under pressure, you would be miserly and it would bring out your malevolence. Here you are then, people who are called upon to spend out in the Way of Allah and then some of you are miserly! But anyone miserly is miserly to himself alone. Allah is the Rich and you are the poor. If you turn away, He will replace you with a people other than you – and they will not be the same as you." (47:37-39)

The reader may perhaps be surprised that, up to this point, we have quoted *hadiths* before the Qur'an regarding the *dunya* and its real nature. Why, it may be asked, did we not begin with *ayats* of the Qur'an? The answer is that the *hadiths* we have mentioned and commented upon are given by way of an introduction to facilitate an understanding of the *ayats* of the Clear Book.

We have already discussed how the life of this lower world is like a game, how it is ephemeral and worthless if a man has no faith. The *Dunya* is just a pastime for the non-believer, distracting him from the Hereafter. The phenomena and material objects of this world are pleasurable and inviting and the lower selves of men cling to them and become covetous of them. When man finds security and reassurance in them and is distracted by them, it is as if these material things become part of a game. Indeed they do become his playthings and the only way he can free himself of them is by means of *iman*: faith.

Have you not seen people who are far removed from faith? How is it, one must ask, that they desire the *Dunya* and are covetous for it? How is it that they glory in what they achieve in it and are saddened by what passes them by? How is it that they place their trust in the *Dunya?* How is it that they rely on it as a support? All of this is game-playing and distraction.

---

1. There are three stages to life: that before birth, that is the unseen, for which man is not held responsible; the second after birth, which is the planting-ground for man; and the third after death, when man reaps the fruits of his actions.

The *ayat* just quoted explains to us, however, how this pastime may be transformed into something serious, how this distraction may be transformed into a project with a goal and an aim. The means to this is *iman* – belief – and *taqwa* – fear of God. It is through *iman* that man obtains his reward and through it too that he finds pleasure in spending for the Cause of Allah and not for that of Shaytan. It is through *iman* that a balance is achieved in life and through it that a believer is able to avoid meanness. It is faith which allows him to realise fully the truth of the Qur'anic indication that he would only be being mean to himself if he were to become a mean person.

Surely it is Allah who grants and bestows. He alone, may He be praised, is capable of making people poor and needy or making them independent and rich. Whenever a believer gives, he is giving to himself in the first instance, since he is bringing this self closer to the pleasure of Allah. When a believer gives, he is opening the door of good to himself. A person who is mean is not in fact withholding from a poor person but withholding from himself as he is failing to open the doors of mercy to himself.

Do *iman* and *taqwa* then mean that people have to give up all property and wealth? Certainly not, for Allah, may He be exalted, "will give you your reward," and "He will not ask you about your wealth". What the *ayat* does is to unlock the chains from around the neck of the believing man and free him from the prison of the *Dunya*, throwing the doors of freedom wide open for him – that freedom which comes with man's devotion to Allah, may He be exalted. It also indicates the punishment of those who resist, who refuse to spend for the sake of Allah and who refuse to break the obstacles and chains of the *Dunya*: "*If you turn away then He will change you for a people other than you*" (47:38): in other words, a people will come who will carry out what has to be done. And Allah has power over everything.

> *"The likeness of the life of this world is that of water which We send down from the sky, which then mingles with the plants of the earth to provide food for both people and animals. Then, when the earth is at its loveliest and takes on its fairest guise and its people think they have it*

34

in their grasp, Our command comes upon it by night or day and We reduce it to dried-out stubble, as though it had not been flourishing only the day before. Thus do We make Our signs plain for people who reflect." (10:24)

Allah makes a likeness of the beauty of the life of the *Dunya* and the speed with which its plants – which Allah has caused to come out of the earth – come up with the water He sends down from the sky. *"It mingles"* with all the different kinds of fruits and vegetables eaten by man and the grass and fodder eaten by animals. *"When the earth is at its loveliest"* refers to its ephemeral beauty and *"takes on its fairest guise"* refers to its hills clothed in dazzling flowers and blossoms of all kinds and colours. *"And its people"*, referring to those who did the sowing and planting, *"think they have it in their grasp"* means that they will be able to reap and harvest it. But as they are thinking this a thunderbolt strikes or a cold and violent wind blows and the leaves wither and the fruit is lost. *"Our command comes upon it by night or day and We reduce it to dried-out stubble"*: that is, dry after being green and fresh. *"As though it had not been flourishing only the day before"*: that is, as if it had not been ready to reap before that moment. Qatada says that the *ayat* means here, *"as if it were not about to yield its blessing."* *"For people who reflect"* refers to those who draw a lesson from the exceedingly fleeting nature of this world, those who inhabit it and are aware of those who are duped by it. They see how others trust in the deceiving promises of the world, how it slips away from them and how, by its nature, it flees from those who seek after it and seeks those who flee from it.[1]

Such is the life of the *Dunya*, nothing of which is in fact possessed by people other than its pleasures and enjoyments – when, that is, they are content with this world, and engrossed in it and unable to see further to what is more noble and more lasting. This is the water which descends from the sky and the plants which absorb and mingle with it and thrive and bloom for a few moments. Its people are proud of it and imagine that it is by their

---

1. Ibn Kathir, *Tafsir*, vol.2, pp. 442-3.

striving and by their will that it has become resplendent. They imagine that they control it, that nothing can change their relationship with respect to it and that no one can take from them this earth and its green fertility. But even as they are filled with this overflowing joy and happiness and this feeling of assurance and trust, *"Our command comes upon it by night or day and We reduce it to dried-out stubble, as though it had not been flourishing only yesterday"* in a flash, utterly overwhelming and destructive. This then is the *Dunya* in which most people become immersed. They end up by losing the Hereafter completely just to attain a tiny part of the pleasure of this world. There is no security in it, no reassurance for its people, no certainty or permanence at all. And no one can possess anything but the minutest portion of it.[1]

> *"Coin for them the likeness of the life of this world. It is like water We send down from the sky and the plants of the earth combine with it. But then it becomes dry chaff scattered by the winds. Allah has complete power over everything."* (18:44)

This gives a picture of something which occurs suddenly and is only short-lived. It is a sign for us – of impermanence and imminent annihilation. When the water descends from the sky it does not form a current and flow but instead the plants of the earth combine with it. In no time they are dry chaff scattered by the winds. In these short phrases, life comes to an end.

This picture of life as something fleeting and transient is emphasised by Allah in His Book in different ways over and over again, but He also describes the nature of a balanced system of belief containing those values which man should devote himself to on earth. It is those values which are permanent and lasting that should merit our attention and concern.

> *"Wealth and sons are the embellishment of the life of this world. But, in your Lord's sight, right actions which are lasting are better rewarded and a better basis for hope."* (18:45)

---

1. Sayyid Qutb, *In the Shade of the Quran*, vol. 3, p. 1775.

Islam does not, of course, forbid taking pleasure in embellishment as long as it lies within the bounds of decency, but this pleasure and beauty and the value they are given must only be considered within the perspective of lasting values. Beauty alone is not a value in itself. It is not permitted for man to measure the value of his life simply on the basis of the pleasure or beauty he experiences in it, for true value and worth must only be accorded to those *"right actions which are lasting"*, namely in man's deeds, his words, and his acts of worship.

Even though man's hopes and aspirations are usually connected to wealth and children, it is in fact these 'right actions' which are *"better rewarded and a better basis for hope"*. It is these latter to which the true heart clings and on which the highest expectations are founded. It is on account of these actions that the believers can anticipate a happy outcome and reward on the Day of Requital.

> *"Know that the life of this world is nothing but a game and a diversion and beautification and boasting among yourselves and trying to outdo each other in wealth and children. It is like the plant-growth after rain which delights the cultivators and then withers and you see it turning yellow, then it becomes broken stubble. In the Next World there is terrible punishment and also forgiveness from Allah and His good pleasure. The life of this world is nothing but the enjoyment of delusion. "(57:19)*

Allah, may He be exalted, disparages and belittles the matter of the life of this world: "Know that the life of this world is no more than a game and a diversion and beautification and a cause of boasting among yourselves and trying to outdo each other in wealth and children." In these words we see how the true nature of the *dunya* manifests for the people who epouse it. Then Allah, may He be exalted, makes a likeness of the life of the *Dunya* by comparing it to a fleeting blossoming, showing it to be a most ephemeral blessing. *"It is like the plant-growth after rain which delights the cultivators."* It is like the rain which comes after people have despaired of its coming. In the same way that cultivators delight in this growth, the unbelievers delight in the life of the *Dunya,* for surely they are the ones who are the most greedy for it and those who most incline towards it. *"Then it withers and you see it turning yellow, then it becomes broken stubble."* This too is a metaphor for things of the *Dunya* which begin young and fresh but then age and finally become decrepit and disfigured. This is like man himself, who at the start of his life is full of vigour and in the prime of his life, fresh, strong and supple, and good to look at, but then when he begins to age his constitution changes, much of his strength disappears and he becomes old and weak, hardly able to move or do anything.

> *"It is Allah who created you from a weak beginning, then after weakness gave you strength, then after strength ordained weakness and grey hair."* (33:53)

This description indicates the ephemerality of the *Dunya*, that it will cease to be and become empty. Its demise is inevitable just as the coming into being of the Hereafter is inevitable. Allah cautions people against becoming engrossed in the affairs of this world and urges man to good action in it.

> *"In the Next World there is terrible punishment and also forgiveness from Allah and His good pleasure. The life of this world is nothing but the enjoyment of delusion."*
> (57:19)

Surely the *dunya* is a fleeting abode of pleasure, sembling and deceiving for those who find their support in it. So beguiled are they that they delight in it to the point of believing that there is no other abode and that there is no ultimate place of return, whereas in fact it is despicable and insignificant in comparison with the Abode of the Hereafter.[1]

As for the words of Allah *"Know that the life of this world is simply a game and a diversion,"* Ibn 'Atiyya says that what is meant by the life of this world in this *ayat* is the way one deals

---

1. Ibn Kathir, *Tafsir*, vol. 4, p. 334.

with the material goods of this world. As for matters of obedience, worship, man's unavoidable needs of subsistence or anything that aids him towards obedience and worship, this is not what is meant here. The "beautification" which Allah mentions refers to any excess which goes beyond the natural adornment inherent in a thing. The "boasting among yourselves" refers to any vain and arrogant behaviour which goes beyond the bounds of normal behaviour. The "trying to outdo each other" is explained in the following words of the *ayat*, namely "in wealth and children."

The picture painted in this example is that of a person who is born and raised, becomes strong, acquires wealth and children and directs his affairs but then begins to decline, gets old and weak, falls ill, suffers the afflictions of sickness and loss of property and power. Then he dies and all his affairs cease. What was his becomes the property of someone else. After that, his physical body in the grave is transformed into earth which is then struck by the rains. Grass then grows, lush and green, over the grave but then it withers, dries and becomes stubble. Then it is dispersed by the wind and finally disappears.

Al-Ghazali says: "Know that the likeness of the people of the *Dunya* and their heedlessness is that of a people who board a ship which later arrives at a luxuriant island. They disembark to replenish their provisions. The captain warns them against staying too long and orders them to remain only as long as is required to get what they need, telling them that he will set sail and leave them behind if they are late. Some of them set about the task immediately and return with alacrity: they get the best and most spacious places on the ship and establish themselves comfortably in them, while those who stay longer have different fates.

The first group are overcome by gazing at the wonderful flowers and blooms, the flowing rivers, the ripe fruits, the jewels and precious minerals of the island, but then they awake from their stupor, rush to the boat, and find their places beneath the others and are all saved.

The second group is like the first except that it seizes hold of some of the jewels, fruits and flowers. But they are unable to give up all they have collected and so they become weighed down by them. Soon the flowers wilt, the fruit perishes and a storm begins to blow up and they are forced to throw away what they had gathered in order to save themselves.

The third group gets caught up in a jungle. They are heedless of the captain's advice and so when they hear the cry to leave and make their way back to the shore they find the boat has already departed. They are left there with all the things they have collected and perish in that land.

The fourth group are so heedless that they disregard the call completely and the boat leaves without them. Some of them are then eaten by wild animals, some lose their way and perish, some die of hunger and some are bitten by snakes.

Such, Imam al-Ghazali says, is the parable of the people of this *Dunya*. They are distracted by getting caught up in their portions of this ephemeral world and are heedless of the eventual outcome of their affair. Al-Ghazali concludes by observing how ugly are those who claim to have insight and intellect while being duped by lumps of gold and silver, or withered plants and fruit – especially when it is clear that these things cannot accompany them beyond their death. And Allah is the Helper.

> *"We made everything on the earth adornment for it so that We could test them to see whose actions are best. We will certainly make everything on it a barren wasteland."*[1] (18:7-8)

Allah informs us that He has made the *Dunya* an ephemeral abode, adorned with a vanishing beauty. He has made it an abode of trial, not an abode of permanent residence. The Messenger, may the peace and blessings of Allah be upon him, said: "Truly this world is sweet and green and Allah has given you responsibility in it so look to what you do. Beware of the *Dunya* and beware of women, for surely the first trial and affliction of the tribe of Israel was regarding women."[2]

---

1. See Ibn Kathir, *Tafsir*, vol. 3, p. 77, in which he explains *sa'idan juruzan* as a region of no benefit in which no plants can grow.

2. See *ayats* 32-46 of *Surat al-Kahf* (The Cave) (18).

Related to this *hadith* which depicts the true nature of the *dunya* is the Qur'anic story of the two men disputing about the matter of wealth and standing in the world.

> *"Cite an example to them of two men. To one of them We gave two gardens of grape-vines and surrounded them with date-palms, putting between them some cultivated land. Both gardens yielded their crops and suffered no loss, and We made a river flow right through the middle of them. One was a man of wealth and property and said to his companion while in debate with him, 'I have more wealth than you, more people under me.' He entered his garden, wronging himself, and said, 'I do not think that this will ever end. I do not think the Hour will ever come. But if I should be sent back to my Lord, I will definitely get something better in return.' His companion, with whom he was debating, said to him, 'Do you reject Him who created you from dust, then from a drop of sperm and then formed you as a man? But he is Allah, my Lord, and I will not make anyone a partner with my Lord. Why, when you entered your garden, did you not say, "As Allah wills; there is no strength but in Allah"? Though you see me with less wealth and children than you, it may be that my Lord will give me better than your garden and send down on yours a fireball from the sky so that morning finds it a sliding heap of dust, or morning finds its water drained into the earth so that you cannot get at it.' All the fruit of his labour was completely destroyed and he woke up wringing his hands, regretting all that he had spent on it. It was a ruin with all its trellises fallen in. He said, 'Oh, if only I had not attributed any partner to my Lord!' There was no group to come to his support, besides Allah, and he was not given any help."* (18:32-42)

The story of the two men and the two gardens is a parable depicting ephemeral values and lasting values. It describes two distinct types of people. The first glories in the beauty of this

41

world and the second glories in Allah, each representing a specific group of people. The owner of the two gardens is an example of a man who is dazzled by his wealth. His blessings make him reckless and proud so that he forgets the Greater Power which holds sway over the decree, the destiny of people – and indeed of life itself. He imagines that those blessings will last forever and will not cease, and that his strength and his standing in the world will never leave him. His companion is an example of a believing man who glories in his faith and who remembers his Lord continually. He is a man who sees Allah's blessing as a proof and indication of the Provider of those blessings and of the One who must necessarily be praised and remembered; and he does not rebel against Him, disbelieve in, or deny Him.

The story begins with the setting of the two gardens, blossoming and resplendent. These two gardens produce grapes and each is surrounded by an enclosure of date-palms, between which are cultivated fields through the middle of which flows a river. This is an uplifting sight, full of abundant life, beauty and wealth. The heart of the owner of the two gardens, however, is filled by the thought of these two gardens and he becomes conceited and self-satisfied when gazing upon them. He feels proud and puffs himself up like a cock. He struts around like a peacock behaving arrogantly and haughtily towards his companion: "I have more wealth than you, more people under me."

Then he goes with his companion to one of the gardens and is filled with vanity. He is filled with self-deceit and forgets Allah, neglecting to thank Him for what He has given him, imagining that these two gardens will never fade away. He denies the Resurrection and the Last Day. And even if such a thing as the Last Day should occur, he thinks he would certainly receive solicitude and preferential treatment. Was he not the owner of the two gardens? Without a doubt his "lordship" would be honoured in the Hereafter ("But if I should be sent back to my Lord, I will definitely get something better in return.") Self-delusion causes people of standing and authority in this world, the leisured and wealthy classes, to believe that the values and norms accorded them by the people of this ephemeral world will also be extended to them even if they should reach the realms of the Higher Assembly.

As for his poor companion, he glories in what is lasting and higher, proud of his beliefs and his faith, proud of Allah the One to whom people bow in humility. *"His companion, with whom he was debating, said to him, 'Do you reject Him who created you from dust?'"* We see from this that the power of faith has been instilled into his believing heart. He is unconcerned with wealth, unconcerned how may persons are under him. He is not duped by riches or self-conceit. He does not falter in his belief in the Real, the Truth, and he does not compromise this Truth when dealing with his companions.

Suddenly the scene changes from that of growth and luxuriance to one of destruction and desolation, from a state of conceit and haughtiness to one of regret and seeking forgiveness. This, in fact, is only what the believing man had anticipated.

> *"All the fruit of his labour was completely destroyed and he woke up wringing his hands, regretting all that he had spent on it. It was a ruin with all its trellises fallen in. He said, 'Oh, if only I had not attributed any partner to my Lord!'"*

And this is an quite dramatic scene. All the fruit have been destroyed and the trellises of the garden have all collapsed and broken in pieces. The owner is clenching his fists, dejected and despondent at his lost wealth and his lost efforts. The curtain comes down upon this desolation; the might and splendour of Allah is seen to descend upon the scene as the strength and power of man is seen to fade and disappear.[1]

> *"To mankind the love of worldly appetites is painted in glowing colours: of women and children, and heaped-up mounds of gold and silver, and horses with fine markings, and livestock, and fertile farmland. All that is merely the enjoyment of the life of this world. But the best homecoming is to the Presence of Allah."* (3:14)

---

1. Sayyid Qutb, *In the Shade of the Quran*, vol. 4, p. 227.

43

In this *ayat* Allah, may He be exalted, states clearly what He has made appealing to those attached to the life of the *Dunya*, namely the various sensual enjoyments associated with women and children, wealth, horses, livestock and land. He begins with women because the trial and temptation associated with them is greatest, as has been established in a sound *hadith* in which the Prophet said, may the peace and blessings of Allah be upon him: "I have not left behind me any trial more harmful to men than women. If however the intention concerning these women is to remain within the bounds of decency and to increase the number of one's children then this is a desirable and worthy intention."

This is confirmed in the *hadiths* which urge men to marry and increase their progeny, for example: "Surely the good in this *Umma* is in those who have the most women". The Prophet, may the peace and blessings of Allah be upon him, also said: "The *Dunya* is enjoyment and the best of this enjoyment is a right-acting woman. When a man looks at her he is filled with joy, when he commands her she obeys and when he is absent she guards herself and his wealth for him." In another *hadith* we read: "Women and perfume evoke love in me and I have been granted coolness of the eye in the prayer." 'A'isha, may Allah be pleased with her, said, "There was nothing dearer to the Messenger of Allah, may the peace and blessing of Allah be upon him, than women, except for horses." And in another narration: "...than horses, except for women."

A man's love of children is sometimes for the sake of showing off and treating them as adornments to his property, in which case it is harmful to him. At other times, however, children are desired in order to increase the Community, to increase the *Umma* of Muhammad, may the peace and blessings of Allah be upon him, to increase the number of those who worship Allah alone with no associate, in which case it is laudable and praiseworthy, indeed even enviable as is clear from the *hadith*: "Marry those who are loving and devoted and who are fertile and prolific, for surely I shall make this community greater than others on the Day of Rising by means of you."

Love of wealth, too, is like this. Sometimes it is for ostentation and conceit and to act arrogantly towards the weak and tyrannically towards the poor, in which case it is to be frowned upon. Sometimes, however, it is in order to spend on one relations, to strengthen family ties, and for acts of kindness and acts of worship and obedience towards Allah, in which case it is praiseworthy and laudable according to the *Shari'a*.

Love of horses may be of three kinds. There are those who keep them fit and ready in preparation for using them for the Cause of Allah: that is, for the moment when they need them to go out on a raid, in which case they are to be praised. There are others, however, who keep them in a reckless and wanton fashion, competing with or even defying the people of Allah, in which case such horses will become a terrible burden for their owners. There are still others who keep them for breeding and to maintain a pure stock, but who do not forget Allah's share in them when they are needed in His Way, in which case these horses become a protecting veil for their owners on the Last Day.

Imam Ahmad relates with his own chain of narration that Abu Dharr, may Allah be pleased with him, recounted: "The Messenger of Allah, may the peace and blessings of Allah be upon him said, "There is not an Arab horse but that it can be heard making two supplications every morning: 'O Allah, surely You have made me a possession of one of the sons of Adam so make me among his dearest of his property, the dearest of the members of his household.'"

The word of Allah "livestock" in the above *ayat* refers to camels, cows and sheep and goats; and "fertile farmland" refers to land used either for planting trees or for sowing crops.

> *"The life of this world is nothing but game-playing and diversion. The Next World is better for those who are godfearing. Will you not then use your intellects?"* (6:33)

The commentators say that His words *"The life of this world is nothing but game-playing and diversion"* means that most of the life of this world is like that. It is a game which will not last, and which has no aim or purpose if it is unaccompanied by faith. I have long reflected on the reality of the life of this world and have found that in itself it does not reveal any aim or purpose of a higher and more sublime kind. It simply consists of food and drink, marriage and merriment, interspersed with sadness and anxieties. I have examined the highest aspirations of man in his world, that is things like real estate which bring profit and income, servants and workers, cars and private planes, luxurious palaces with appointed air-conditioned rooms; but then one must ask what is the outcome of all this.

Every man will die and must necessarily leave whatever he has acquired to someone else. But what has he gained for himself? He has lived out his days eating and drinking but in doing so has merely lived the life of an animal – unless he has remained within the bounds of faith. Allah, may He be exalted, says, describing the state of those who disbelieve: *"They eat as cattle eat, and the Fire will be their eventual abode."* (47:12) For this reason we see that a man without faith has no value. He achieves no purpose whatsoever by his existence: *"Leave them to eat and enjoy themselves. Let false hope divert them. They shall soon know."* (15: 3)

They will leave behind them their palaces; their objects of luxury will fall into disuse, as will the pastimes and amusements; all will be lost and disappear. Nothing will remain but desolation, the darkness of the grave, an empty record, a difficult reckoning, eternal anxiety and a painful torment.

Faith alone is the means to saving oneself for it is through faith that the grave is illuminated and becomes a meadow of the Garden. It is by right action that the Record is rectified, the Reckoning made easy, and eternal happiness takes the place of everlasting terror. It is clear that the abode of the Hereafter is better for those who are god-fearing. So why, one may well ask, do people not use their intelligence!

"Among His signs is that He created you from dust and here you are now, human beings dispersed throughout the earth. Among His signs is that He created partners for you of your own kind so that you might find repose with them, and placed affection and compassion between you. There are certainly signs in that for people who reflect. Among

46

*His signs is the creation of the heavens and the earth and
the great variety of your languages and colours. There are
certainly signs in that for every being. Among His signs is
your sleep by night and day and your seeking after His
unbounded favour. There are certainly signs in that for
people who hear. Among His signs are that He shows you
lightning, a source of fear and eager hope, and sends
down water from the sky, bringing the earth to life by it
when it was dead. There are certainly signs in that for
people who use their intellects. Among His signs is that
heaven and earth hold firm by His command. Then, when
He calls you forth from the earth, you will emerge at once.
Everyone in the heavens and the earth belongs to Him. All
are submissive to Him."*

(30:19-25)

This succession of *ayats* shows the *Dunya* to be a place of
meanings. The *ayats* demonstrate that, with understanding, one
may transform this world into a means, a riding beast for getting
closer to Allah, may He be blessed and exalted. Reflect upon the
ayats and the way that they form a sequential commentary on the
state of man! First to be mentioned is our creation from dust and
how we have been dispersed throughout the world; then comes the
creation of mates for us in which lies tranquillity, love and mercy;
then the difference in our languages, colours and states; then our
sleep both during the day and the night; then our constant striving
for the bounty of Allah – in this both believer and non-believer are
equal.

Next comes an *ayat* concerning the clouds. When the lightning
contained within them is seen by man it inspires fear in him, as
does the thunder. But it also arouses a feeling of "eager hope" in
anticipation of the rains and subsequent fertility as the water
revives the earth after its death-like dormancy. Then there is the
great *ayat* indicating the ordering of the heavens and the earth
which "hold firm by His command" followed by the indication of
the great power involved in reviving the dead. Finally comes the
ayat indicating the submission of everything to Allah, may He be
exalted: all submit to Him irrespective of whether they are believ-

ers or non-believers. This sequence of *ayats* activates the intellect and revives the mind.

> *"We created above you seven levels, and We were not heedless of Creation. We sent down a measured amount of water from heaven and lodged it firmly in the earth; and We are quite capable of taking it away. By means of it We produce gardens of dates and grapes for you, in which there are many fruits for you and from which you eat, and a tree springing forth from Mount Sinai yielding oil and seasoning to those who eat it. And there is certainly a lesson for you in your livestock. We give you to drink from what is in their bellies and there are many ways in which you benefit from them, and some of them you eat; and you are conveyed on them and on ships as well."* (40:17-22)

These *ayats* permit the believer to make a brief survey of the heights of creation, of the essential activities of human life and the means to achieving them, and of the immediate concerns and requirements of man. It produces a widening of the sphere of perception of the believer.

There are seven levels above him. Water descends from the sky, gathers in the earth but does not evaporate quickly. Allah would be quite capable of causing it to disappear. As He says in *Surat al-Mulk*, *"Say: Do you not see? If one morning your water were to disappear into the earth, who would then bring you running water?"* (67:30). When the believer reads this *ayat* he should say to himself: "Allah, the Lord of the Worlds!" as an expression of praise, of recognition of the generosity of his Lord. There are different kinds of gardens, date palms, vines and fruits, and there are different kinds of livestock which are subservient to man and which he uses as food or as mounts.

> *"Man need only look at his food. We pour down water in torrents, then split the earth in furrows and make grain grow in it; and grapes and herbs; and olives and dates; and luxuriant gardens; and fruit and pastureland: for you and your livestock to enjoy."* (80:24-32)

Who causes the water to descend from the sky? Who splits open the earth? Who allows it to be tilled and facilitates germination? Who causes the plants, the trees and the fruits to grow? Surely it is Allah, may He be exalted. He did not cause the water to come down in response to a command from man. The earth was not made subservient out of obedience to the sons of Adam. Rather Allah has facilitated these things for us so that we might enjoy them and draw a lesson from their creation.

Look at the beginning and end of these *ayats*. To introduce the subject, He says: *"Man only has to look at his food ..."* and at the end *"for you and your livestock to enjoy."* The relation between them should stimulate us to think. Indeed, reflection on this matter is incumbent on any man of intellect. It is inevitable that any person who reflects deeply will seek salvation upon reading these *ayats* for they raise him beyond any association with animals and beyond being content with mere bestial pleasure. Surely any man of intellect must, by means of faith and investigation, raise himself upwards, towards the Hereafter.

> *"Are you stronger in frame or is the sky? He built it. He raised its vault, levelled it, and made its night dark and brought forth its morning light. Next He smoothed out the earth, and brought forth from it its water and its pastureland, and He fixed the mountains firm: for you and for your livestock to enjoy."* (79:27-33)

When man reflects upon the *ayats* of the Generous Qur'an, especially those *ayats* which stress his dependence upon these archetypal creational realities, he may well imagine that his life's work consists in awakening his intellect. Indeed these *ayats* raise the believer's vision from the realm of the mere material to a world in which the beauty, purpose and aim of creation become evident. This is the true function of the intellect: reflection upon the heavens and the precision with which everything works; reflection upon the night and all the phenomena associated with it; reflection upon the earth which Allah has spread out for us and upon the way water springs from it and returns to it, by means of which all aspects of life are sustained; and reflection upon the stabilizing mountains which keep the earth in place.

All these things contribute to the "enjoyment" mentioned by Allah. What is surprising, however, is that these *ayats* close with the recognition that the enjoyment of pleasure is common to both man, who possesses intellect, and the beasts, which are incapable of rational reflection. This recognition also acts as an admonition. The Muslim must necessarily distinguish between this "enjoyment" which is a natural part of creation and the excessive pursuit of enjoyment for enjoyment's sake. To realise this distinction his intellect must comprehend the loss which is the lot of the non-believer who becomes fixated in his pursuit of the ephemeral pleasure of this world.

> *"O Mankind! Eat what is good and lawful on the earth. And do not follow in the footsteps of Shaytan. He is your clear-cut enemy. He only commands you to evil and indecency and to say something about Allah that you do not know."* (2:167-168)

> *"O you who believe! Eat of the good things We have provided for you and show thanks to Allah, if you worship Him alone."* (2:171)

The aspiration of the believer must always be directed towards the good things. It is an impulse which urges him to emulate whatever is high and sublime. But it is not just believers who are referred to here. The Lord, may He be praised, is the Lord of all mankind, the King of all mankind, the God of all mankind. The above *ayat* begins with a call to everyone: "O Mankind!" The second *ayat* is directed to the believers in particular. What is remarkable is the different way in which the matter is dealt with in the two *ayats*. In the first case, directed to mankind in general, that is, to both the believers and the non-believers, Allah, may He be exalted, says: *"Eat what is good and lawful on the earth."* The command that mankind should seek what is good and to avoid what is evil is general in this instance. In the second *ayat*, directed at the believers, the command is connected to belief. Allah, may

He be exalted, says: *"Eat of the good things We have provided for you and show thanks."* Good things have been decreed as provision for the believers, as if they were restricted to them. Then a comparison is made between the matter of eating good things and the matter of giving thanks for this provision.

This reminds one of the words of Allah, may He be exalted: *"Say: 'Who has forbidden the fine clothing of Allah and the good kinds of provision He has produced for His slaves?' Say: 'On the Day of Rising such things will be exclusively for those who believed during the life of this world.'"* (7:30) The good things belong primarily to the believers, both in this world and the Next; and non-believers only share in them on an incidental basis in this world and have no share in them in the Next World. This is the meaning gleaned on examination of the two above mentioned *ayats*. Allah, may He be exalted, reminds us in both texts that He has permitted mankind to eat the things of the earth because it is, by its nature, *halal*, that is sanctioned by Allah since it is good and wholesome to eat; that is, it is good in itself and not harmful to the body or the intellect. He reminds us that He has forbidden us from following in the steps of Shaytan – that is, in the ways and paths by which Shaytan leads those who follow him astray, leads them to, for example, the superstitious practice of designating certain camels as *bahira* or *sa'iba* or *wasila*, thereby dedicating them to false gods, instead of accepting them as a source of beauty and benefit.

Likewise in a *hadith* from 'Iyad ibn Himar, in the *Sahih* of Muslim, it is related from the Messenger of Allah, may the peace and blessings of Allah be upon him, that He said that Allah, may He be exalted, has declared: "Any wealth that I have bestowed upon My slaves is *halal* for them" and "I have created My slaves on the pure true Way and then Shaytan came to them and he misled them from their *deen* and he made *haram* for them what I had made *halal* for them".

The *hafidh* Abu Bakr ibn Mardawayh relates from Ibn 'Abbas that he said: "I recited this *ayat* in front of the Prophet, may the peace and blessings of Allah be upon him: 'O people, eat of what is in the earth which is *halal* and wholesome,' and then Sa'd ibn

51

Abi Waqqas stood up saying: 'O Messenger of Allah, call on Allah so that He answer my supplications,' to which he replied: "O Sa'd: 'Make your food wholesome and your prayers will be answered, by the One who has the self of Muhammad in His hand. Surely a man does not cast a morsel of *haram* food into his belly without his prayers remaining unanswered for forty days and the Fire is more fitting for any slave whose meat comes from ill-gotten property or usury.'"

What Allah is saying is that He is commanding His slaves, His believing slaves, to eat of the good things that He has bestowed on them and that they should thank Him for these good things if they are truly His slaves. He is saying that eating only what is *halal* is a prerequisite for the acceptance of supplications and worship, just as the eating what is *haram* prevents these supplications and worship from being accepted. It has been narrated in the *hadith* related by Imam Ahmad from Abu Hurayra that the Messenger of Allah said, may the peace and blessings of Allah be upon him: "O people, surely Allah is good and He only accepts what is good. Allah has commanded the believers to do the same things as He has commanded the Messengers, saying: 'O you who believe, eat of the good things with which We have provided you.'" Then he mentioned a man on a long journey, his hair dishevelled and dusty, who stretches his hands to the sky saying: "O Lord, O Lord!" when his food is *haram* and his drink is *haram* and his clothes are, so that he is in fact nurtured and nourished on the *haram*. How can his supplication be answered when he is in that state?[1]

> *"Anyone who acts rightly, male or female, being a believer, We will give them a good life and We will recompense them according to the best of what they did."*
>
> (16:97)

> *"Allah coins a likeness of a city which was safe and at peace, its provision coming to it plentifully from every side. Then it showed ingratitude for Allah's blessings so Allah made it bear the robes of hunger and fear for what it did."* (16:112)

---

1. Ibn Kathir, *Tafsir*, vol. 1, pp. 209-211.

There is a promise from Allah, may He be exalted, to anyone who acts rightly, or, in other words, acts in accordance with the Book of Allah, may He be exalted, and the *Sunna* of His Messenger, may the peace and blessings of Allah be upon him, no matter whether they are male or female, just as long as their hearts believe in Allah and His Messenger. Right action is commanded and set down in the *Shari'a* by Allah, and in return He will give the person a good life in this *Dunya* and will reward them with better than their actions deserve in the Hereafter.

A "good life" implies all kinds of ease. Ibn 'Abbas, may Allah be pleased with him and his father, relate that it refers to provision which is *halal* and good. According to 'Ali, may Allah be pleased with him, it means contentment. It is also narrated of Ibn 'Abbas that he said that it refers to happiness as well. According to ad-Dahhak it means *halal* provision and worship. The correct interpretation is that the good life includes all these things.

The Prophet, may the peace and blessings of Allah be upon him, said: "Those who submit and who are given sufficient provision and whom Allah makes content with what He has given them are the successful ones." He also said, may the peace and blessings of Allah be upon him, "Surely Allah does not let go to waste a single good action which He bestows upon a believer in the *Dunya* or gives as a reward in the *Akhira*. But in the case of the unbeliever, He causes his good actions to be consumed in the *Dunya* so that when he proceeds to the Hereafter not a single good action remains for which He can accord good."[1]

> *"How many wrongdoing cities We destroyed, and now all their roofs and walls are fallen in; and abandoned wells and tall stuccoed towers!"* (22:45)

> *"How many wrongdoing cities I allowed time to, and then I seized them. The final destination is to Me!"*
> (22:48)

Wrongdoing is a wide-open door to destruction and even if in the case of the wrongdoing of an individual his destruction is

---

1. Ibn Kathir, *Tafsir*, vol. 2, p. 634.

reserved for the Hereafter, it does not necessarily mean that in the case of the wrongdoing of the community as a whole its punishment will be delayed until the Next World. In fact punishment is frequently meted out to a community which is responsible for, or condones, wrongdoing. This is in addition to the punishment of the Next World awaiting those who actually take part in wrongdoing.

The above *ayats* are from *Surat al-Hajj,* and the *ayat* containing the statement about the destruction of the wrongdoing city precedes the one in which Allah talks of allowing time before seizing them. Because of the way that one *ayat* precedes the other, one senses the warning of the fate awaiting the wrongdoing community. It is as if this mention of allowing them time – coming as it does later in the *sura* – to ensure that wrongdoers are not lulled into a false sense of security by this delay.

The reasons and causes which bring this destruction down upon a city are all to be found in a people's wrongdoing. This is a general phenomenon which can exist in every aspect of a community. In the first instance it has to do with faith. Wrongdoing with respect to people's beliefs is *shirk*: that is, making other gods, powers or other things partners with Allah. He says, may He be exalted: *"Surely associating something else with Him is wrongdoing."* (31:13) There is also the wrongdoing and oppression that occur with respect to social laws, economic laws or cultural practices and the inevitable result of such wrongdoing is ruin and destruction. The wells are abandoned despite the tall stuccoed towers.

Reflect upon the things that cause a society to perish. Implied in the abandoning of the wells is that they have dried up and therefore that agricultural production and other sources of income and revenue have ceased. One may find an analogy today in factories which cease production entirely or in which production is severely hampered or complicated, or all of whose energy and power is channelled into producing something which is of no benefit. But it is also the case, of course, that the springs which irrigate today's modern farms may become depleted and peter out with the result that fields and land become uncultivable[1].

---

1. Some farmers also change their productive lands into building plots or sell the earth and clay to brick factories and engage in other destructive activities.

The tall stuccoed towers are a sign of tyrannical luxury and destructive extravagance. The fact that the weights and balances of the marketplace become defective, that the means of life cease to function properly, and that houses fall into ruin is directly related to the fact that enormous palaces are also being built. Can normal life continue in circumstances where luxury and tyranny reign?

"Great corruption has appeared in both land and the sea because of what people's own hands have earned so they may taste something of what they have done and so that perhaps they will return." (30:40)

This *ayat* highlights a certain aspect of life, namely corruption and degeneration, in order to manifest an important truth: only faith and trust in Allah guarantee mankind happiness in the Next World, just as only faith and trust can guarantee Allah's contentment and provide a firm basis for action and behaviour in the *Dunya*. People who transgress and rebel against the laws of God lose the happiness of the Hereafter and will find no security or firm foundation in the life of this world.

Corruption manifests itself because of people's behaviour. One must remember how scientific inventions and the associated levels of comfort and luxury they have brought to people have, in their essence, inflicted enormous harm. The environment has been polluted and the atmosphere has been filled with impurities. One has only to consider how the ozone layer of the stratosphere has been eaten away by poisonous gases. It is precisely this layer which protects life on earth from the onslaught of infra-red rays, from all the dangerous and destructive elements found in the various atmospheric layers which have an effect on life and may in the end destroy it.

Man creates and invents and the more he masters the laws of existence the more kinds of benefit his inventions provide. But then this activity rebounds back on him in the form of corruption, pollution and imbalances in day-to-day life. Diseases appear, social and economic difficulties intensify, and calamities and natural disasters proliferate. Instead of disappearing, however, the problems and dangers increase. Despite this man goes on with his research unconcerned about the difficulties which appear as a result of it. The beginning of *Surat ar-Rahman* comes to mind in this context.

> *"The All-Merciful taught the Qur'an. He created man and taught him expression. The sun and moon both run with precision. The stars and trees all bow down in prostration. He erected heaven and established the balance, so that you would not overstep in the balance. Give just weight; do not skimp in the balance."* (55:1-7)

The surprising thing is that the word "balance" occurs three times. The first time it comes is *"He erected heaven and established the balance"*: and this refers to the laws which govern the heavens, as when Allah, may He be exalted, says: *"and He inspired each sky with its affair."* After this comes the prohibition *"...so that you would not overstep in the balance"* and thereafter *"do not skimp in the balance"*. *"So that you would not overstep"* means that although man has a tendency to covet he must not transgress the natural laws and subject them to his will in such a way as to manipulate them for something that Allah has not created them for.

Part of the greatness and vastness of Islam is that it contains the wisdom of limitation. Allah has explained, may He be praised, that man will discover laws and will try to master them for his own benefit, or at least what he considers to be for his own benefit. The Qur'an, however, cautions against this. Consider, for example, the splitting of the atom. Was that not a transgression of natural law? What are we to think of 'star wars' technology and its implications for the fate of man? Is that too not an overstepping of the bounds? Genetic engineering, interference in the sphere of embryology, the modification of hereditary characteristics, the poisoning of the atmosphere and the seas, lakes and rivers – all of these things, and many others as well, indicate that the natural balance has been upset. This in turn leads to a general corruption, manifesting both on the land and sea because of the actions of man.

As for Allah's prohibition against "skimping in the balance", this indicates the total prohibition of usury and improper practices in the market-place.

> "They also said, 'We have more wealth and children. We are not going to be punished.' Say: 'My Lord expands provision to anyone He wills and also restricts it, yet the majority of mankind do not know.' It is not your wealth or your children that will bring you near to Us, except in the case of people who believe and act rightly. Such people will have a double recompense for what they did. They will be safe from all harm in the High Halls of Paradise."
>
> (34:35-37)

The *Dunya* in itself is not a means whereby man can draw closer to Allah, may He be exalted. There are those, described above, who have lost their prospects for the Hereafter and there are those, in contrast, who believe and act rightly. The former have been thrown into the chasm of Hell through their disbelief and have been caught up in the snares of this world. Their souls have been beguiled by the world. The world becomes the only thing they recognise and their hearts submit to it. The world has tricked and duped them with its enticements to such an extent that they have become slaves to it. The gates of its beauty have been opened for them and they have fallen passionately in love with this beauty, so much so that they say "We have more wealth and children".

When they feel the pleasurable sensations connected with wealth and being in control of it, when they experience the delight of ownership and all the feelings of pride and superiority associated with it, they say, "We will not be punished," even though the *ayat* makes it plain to them that provision is from Allah, that it is He who expands it for whomever He wills and that it is He who restricts it for whomever He wills. The *ayat* concludes the matter by saying: "*It is not your wealth or your children that will bring you near to Us,*" as wealth and children are not a door to the pleasure of Allah, may He be exalted.

Then the exception to this rule is emphasized with respect to faith: *"except in the case of people who believe and act rightly."* Thus it is by means of faith – *iman* – that the game and distraction that is this world is transformed into something serious, its beauty and allure into something rewarding and a blessing. *"Such people shall have a double recompense,"* that is, any action or act of generosity will be doubly rewarded; and then *"They will be safe from all harm in the High Halls of Paradise"*.

In a hadith from Abu Kabsha al-Anmari we read: "Surely the *dunya* is for four kinds of people: one on whom Allah has bestowed wealth and knowledge – he is the one who has fear of his Lord in this world and who maintains the ties of kinship and recognises the rights of Allah in this world – and this is the best of stations; someone on whom Allah has bestowed knowledge but not wealth but who has a sound intention and says, 'If I had wealth I would do as such and such a person does,' and that being his intention he is rewarded in the same way as the other; one whom Allah has provided with wealth but not knowledge – he uses the wealth rashly and recklessly without knowledge and without fear of his Lord, he does not maintain good family relations, and does not recognise the rights Allah has over him – and that is the most despicable of stations; finally there is someone whom Allah has not provided with wealth or knowledge and who says, 'If I possessed wealth then I would act as such a such a person (who has),' and that being his intention the burden of their wrong actions will count as the same."[1]

The above *hadith* explains the different categories of people in the *Dunya*. There are two kinds who have success: people with wealth and knowledge who spend their wealth knowledgeably. Then there are those who have been given knowledge but not wealth, although they wish they had what the others have in order to act in the same manner as them and spend for the sake of Allah. In the case of these two, the reward is the same.

But there are also two kinds doomed to destruction. Those who possess wealth but do not use it with knowledge – ignorant people who act recklessly and stupidly with their wealth. And finally

---

1. According to at-Tirmidhi this is a good and sound *hadith*.

there are those who have been given neither wealth nor knowledge but who wish they had wealth so as to behave recklessly with it just as the others do. These two will suffer the same punishment for their wrong action.

So reflect – may Allah guide you – upon the excellence of knowledge together with wealth, and upon the excellence of correct intention together with knowledge. Be careful also – may Allah protect you – that you are not among those with wealth but no knowledge or those who have a base intention without wealth or knowledge, lest you become one of those doomed to destruction. If you are not a person of knowledge then keep the company of those who have knowledge and ask them and reflect with understanding upon the *deen*. Then it may be that you will become one of the successful. I ask Allah for health and strength for myself and for all of you.

> *"As for those who reject, even if they had everything on the earth, and the same again with it, to ransom themselves from the punishment of the Day of Rising, it would not be accepted from them. They will have a painful punishment."* (5: 38)

Such, then, is the reality of the *Dunya* and this is its true worth in the eyes of those who understand and reflect. On the Day of Resurrection the whole of it will not even make up a ransom for those who might want to offer it as one; all of the contents of the world will be of no value. It is narrated from Anas ibn Malik that the Messenger of Allah, may the peace and blessings of Allah be upon him, said: "A man of the people of the Fire will be brought and will be asked: 'O son of Adam, how do you find your couch?' and he will answer, 'The worst of couches!' And then he will be asked, 'Would you ransom (your release) in return for the earth's weight in gold?' and he will reply, 'Yes, O Lord.' Then Allah, may He be exalted, will say, 'You lie! I asked you for a lesser amount than this and you did not do it.' Then the man is consigned to the Fire."

Allah informs us that the unbelievers will be fuel for the Fire. All that has been given them in the *Dunya* – by way wealth and children - will be of no benefit to them in the eyes of Allah. It will not save them from the painful torment. Allah, may He be exalted, says in *Surat at-Tawba*:

> *"Do not let their wealth and children impress you. Allah merely wants to punish them by them during their life in this world, and for their souls to depart while they are still rejectors."* (9:55)

And in *Surat Ali 'Imran*:

> *"Do not be misled by the fact that the people who reject move freely about the earth. A brief enjoyment; then their shelter will be Jahannam. What an evil resting-place!"* (3:196-7)

Allah's words "the people who reject" refer to those who reject the *ayats* of Allah, who deny His Messengers, who oppose His Book and who in no way benefit from the revelation of His Prophets.

> *"As for those who reject, their wealth and children will not avail them against Allah in any way. They are the fuel of the Fire."* (3:10)

It is narrated from 'A'isha that she said that the Messenger of Allah, may the peace and blessings of Allah be upon him, said: "This world is the home of those who have no home, and things are stored up and accumulated for it only by those who have no intellect."[1]

How can people take the *Dunya* as their home when they are all the time travelling away from it? Why do they spend so much energy gathering things together when they are only going to have to abandon them? This *hadith* evokes both man's tendency to greed and covetousness and also his impulse to salvation. Those

---

1. This is related in the *Majmu'at az-Zawa'id* by Ahmad – and his transmitters are of the *sahih* rank except for Duwayd who has the rank of trustworthy.

who truly want the best for themselves will not take the *Dunya* as their home and in the same way people who really desire happiness will store up good actions for the Hereafter and for the Garden.

It is narrated by Ibn Hatim and Ibn Mardawayh from Umm al-Fadl (the mother of 'Abdullah ibn 'Abbas) that the Messenger of Allah, may the peace and blessing of Allah be upon him, stood up one night in Makka and said, "Have I delivered the message?", repeating it three times. Then 'Umar ibn al-Khattab got up and cried out: "O Allah! Yes! You have made a great endeavour, you have striven and you have given advice and admonition, so have patience!" Then the Prophet replied, may the peace and blessing of Allah be upon him, "May faith become so manifest that disbelief will return to its own abode and may the men of the seas immerse themselves in Islam. A time will certainly come to people when they will read the Qur'an, implement what it says, teach its teachings, and say: 'We have learned and so who is there better than us?' but there will be no good in them." They said: "O Messenger of Allah, who are those people?" He replied: "They will be from amongst you and they will be fuel for the Fire."[1]

Ibn Kathir relates this from Ibn Mardawayh and then he narrates it through Musa ibn 'Ubayda from Muhammad ibn Ibrahim from the daughter of al-Had from al-'Abbas ibn 'Abd al-Muttalib with the same text.

It is narrated from al-Mustawrid that the Messenger of Allah, may the peace and blessings of Allah be upon him, said: "This world is nothing in comparison to the Hereafter. It is like someone who dips his finger into the sea – let him see how much clings to it."[2]

---

1. Ibn Kathir, *Tafsir*, vol. 1, p. 363.
2. At-Tirmidhi reports this and describes it as a good and sound *hadith*.

You can see just how delicate is the state of equilibrium between the *Dunya* and the *Akhira*. The need for the believer to maintain this balance of perspective is affirmed by the Generous Qur'an, as we have seen above, and this *hadith* explains the true nature of the *Dunya* using another metaphor. If someone were to put his finger in the ocean, would whatever clings to his finger even be enough to slake the thirst of a parched throat? Would there even be enough on his finger to dampen a sheet of paper or enough to wash off even the smallest of spots? No, there would not be enough for any of these things. This, then, is the reality of the *dunya* and fools are they who would cling to it. It is the Hereafter that is clearly the real abode of riches, of power, of meaning and substance, and of ever-renewed gifts. The man of intellect is he who works for that which goes on forever during his stay in this ephemeral world which is doomed to disappear.

> Muslim, Tirmidhi and Nasa'i narrate from al-Mustawrid ibn Shaddad who reported the Messenger, may the peace and blessings of Allah be upon him, as having said, "By Allah, in the Hereafter the *Dunya* will seem like nothing but one of you dipping his finger in the ocean and looking to see what clings to it." The Messenger, may the peace and blessings of Allah be upon him, also said, "A tiny pool of water in the Garden is better than this world and all that is in it."

If a tiny pool of water in the Garden is worth more than the *Dunya*, then it is clear that if there is anything equal in worth to the *Dunya* it will never be greater in significance than this tiny pool. According to al-Qurtubi, this is similar to Allah's words: "Say: 'The pleasures of this world are few.'" This in no way exalts or accords significance to these pleasurable things for they are only pleasurable in themselves and in relation to this world, whereas in relation to the Next World they have little or no worth or significance. The Prophet thus expresses this idea by way of a simile and as a comparison, there being, strictly speaking, no relation between the finite and the infinite. This he indicates with the words "and looking to see what clings to it". What he means by this is that the amount of salt-water remaining on the finger is of absolutely no value just as the *Dunya* is of no value in relation to the Next World, the water remaining on the finger representing the *Dunya* and the rest of the ocean, the Next World.[1]

> Ibn 'Umar narrates that the Messenger of Allah, may the peace and blessings of Allah be upon him, said: "Two ferocious wolves in an animal-pen eating the livestock and causing mayhem are not more harmful than are love of glory and love of wealth to the *deen* of a Muslim man."[2]

So these two aspects of the reality of the life of the *Dunya* represent a major danger to a person's faith. Love of reputation and position make a believer covetous for this world, predispose him to showing off, to being excessively obsequious with people and to striving to maintain his rank amongst them. Love of wealth drives a man to lying, treachery, trickery and deceit and causes him to ignore the obligations which accompany his possession of wealth, with the result that he neither pays *zakat* nor gives *sadaqa*. Love of wealth and rank certainly are like are two hungry wolves. If they enter into a believer's heart they bring about the destruction of his *deen* and put an end to his faith, just as two hungry wolves would devour sheep and goats.

> Ibn 'Abbas, may Allah be pleased with him and his father, relates that the Messenger of Allah observed, may the peace and blessing of Allah be upon him: "There are two blessings which many people deceive themselves into ignoring: health and rest."[3] In the narration of ad-Darimi the text reads: "Surely health and rest are two of the blessings of Allah."

---

1. See *Fath al-Bari*, vol. 11, pp. 236-237.
2. Al-Bazzar narrates this in *Majmu'at az-Zawa'id* - and the narration of Ibn al-'Ala', a trustworthy person is contained in it; the rest of the narrators are also trustworthy.
3. *Al-Fath al-Bari*, vol. 11, pp. 233-4.

Ibn Battal says that the meaning of the *hadith* is that a man will not find rest until he has sufficient for his needs and his body is healthy. Whoever has these two things should make sure that he does not give short measure to himself by omitting to thank Allah for what He has bestowed upon him. One way of thanking Him is to obey His commands and to avoid what He has forbidden. Anyone who falls short in this respect is tricking himself. The Prophet, peace and blessings be upon him, has indicated by the words "many people" that few people are in harmony with this truth.

According to Ibn Jawzi, many a time a person is healthy but has no rest or leisure because he is busy earning his living; and many a time he is wealthy and independent but is not healthy. If the two are combined, then laziness dominates him, obedience ceases and he is cheated. The upshot of this is that the *dunya* is the seed-bed of the Hereafter and in it there is trade whose profit will become manifest in the Next World. Those who use their free time and their health in acts of obedience to Allah will enjoy happiness, but those who use it for acts of disobedience to Allah will be cheating themselves, for work comes after rest, illness after health, then finally old age and death.

At-Tayyibi says that the Messenger, may the peace and blessings of Allah be upon him, is here giving a parable of the responsible individual. He is like a trader with capital who desires profit and also wants to retain the full amount of his original capital. The method he should employ in this business is to investigate who he is dealing with. He must be vigilant so as not to be cheated. Health and leisure are likewise capital so it is incumbent upon him to treat them as an efficient trader would, trading with Allah in the best possible manner so as to obtain, by means of his faith and by opposing his lower self and the enemies of the *deen*, the good both of this world and the Next. Allah Himself uses the same metaphor in *Surat as-Saffat.*

"O you who believe! Shall I direct you to a transaction which will save you from a painful punishment? That you believe in Allah and His Messenger and do jihad *in the*

Way of Allah with your wealth and yourselves. That is bet-
ter for you if you did but know." (61:10-11)

To this purpose we must avoid capitulating to our lower selves
or to the intrigues of Shaytan lest we lose our capital or our profit.
The Prophet's words, indicating that many people cheat themselves with regard to the two matters of leisure and health, are like
the words of Allah *"and few of My slaves are grateful."* (34:13)
The "many people" referred to in the *hadith* corresponds directly
to the few mentioned in the *ayat.*

Qadi Abu Bakr ibn al-'Arabi says that there is a difference of
opinion as to which of Allah's blessings was the first to be
bestowed on His slaves. Some say that it is faith, others that it is
life, and still others that it is health. The first of these, however, is
more likely since this ranks as an absolute blessing and life and
health are two worldly blessings which are not to be counted as
real and true blessings unless they are accompanied by faith. If
they are not, then many are those who will be deceived and cheated: that is, they will lose their profit or it will be diminished.

People who allow their lower selves free rein to command to
what is evil, who incline to constant rest and repose, and who no
longer persevere in maintaining the *hudud* – the parameters of
legitimate behaviour – and in performing acts of obedience, cheat
and deceive themselves and will be judged accordingly.

Chapter Four
Love of the *Dunya* and its Significance

The significance of clinging to this world

The *ayats* quoted below explain the danger of clinging to the *dunya*. It is imperative for us to reflect upon them. The lessons to be drawn from them will help us harvest the fruit contained in them. We must read them with understanding and true acceptance and so that we will be able to act upon them and imitate the example set by them. Allah alone is the Guide to the Straight Path.

The *ayats* from *Surat Yunus* give us a description of the people of the Fire – may Allah give us refuge from it! The first quality of the people of the Fire is that they do not look forward to meeting Allah. Moreover they do not carry out their actions for His sake. It is clear that if they really did anticipate meeting Him they would certainly perform correct actions for His sake. Secondly they are content with the life of this world. Any eagerness and endeavour for what lies beyond it is in their case of a very restricted nature. They expend all their energy in trying to obtain the pleasures, delights and sensual stimulations of this world. They find reassurance and security in what they obtain from this world. They come to rely on it and exult in it. Thirdly they are heedless of the *ayats* of Allah and of how they should awaken themselves to their import. They become completely submerged in the here and now and beguiled by the ephemeral and fleeting. The course of their lives is towards the Fire.

The *ayats* from *Surat Ibrahim* are of deep significance. Those who prefer the life of this world to that of the Hereafter will inevitably be among the party of those who put obstacles in the way of Allah and desire to make His way crooked and tortuous for others. Those who prefer the life of the *Dunya* to the Hereafter do not like the concerns of the *deen* because of the duties it imposes on them. Those who prefer the life of this world naturally tend to abandon everything for the sake of sensual pleasures, irrespective of whether they are *halal* or *haram* – without any limits. It is obvious that this is a barrier and obstacle to the Cause of Allah, whether those concerned are aware of it or not.

People attached to the *Dunya* and the lovers of the *Dunya* invariably have a dislike and hate for the Next World and are heedless of it. They actively engage in opposition to the Way of Allah and they interfere in it, preventing others from gaining access to it. They refrain from helping the believers and make war on those who are committed to establishing the *deen,* harrying the godfearing both secretly and openly.

The *ayats* of *Surat al-An'am* represent a warning for the believers. They command them to leave those who have become beguiled by the life of this world, to separate themselves from those who have found their security and reassurance in it, to abandon those who exult in it because they treat their *deen* as a game and a trivial affair. The *ayats* command them to persevere in remembrance and teaching so that people will not be seized suddenly and unawares, "so that they may warn those who are alive and the Word may be proven against the disbelievers."

The *ayats* from *Surat al-Jathiya* describe the state of those who love this world and who remain beguiled by it until the Day of Raising Up; as a result they become forgetful and heedless.

We shall now turn to these *ayats* in order to read them with full realisation of their import. Ponder them deeply and open your heart to the full sense of their indications.

> *"As for those who do not expect to meet Us and are content with the life of this world and at rest in it, and those who are unmindful of Our signs, the shelter of such people will be the Fire on account of what they earned."*
>
> (10:7-8)

> *"Woe to the rejectors because of a terrible punishment: those who prefer the life of this world to the Next World,*

*and bar access to the way of Allah, wanting to make it
crooked. They are greatly misguided." (14:3-4)*

*"Abandon those who have turned their deen into a game
and a distraction and whom the life of this world has
deluded. Remind by it to prevent a person from being
delivered up to destruction for what he has earned, for he
has no protector or intercessor besides Allah. Were he to
offer every kind of compensation, it would not be accepted
from him. Such people are delivered up to destruction for
what they have earned. They will have scalding water to
drink and a painful punishment on account of their rejection." (6:70)*

*"It will be said, 'Today We have forgotten you as you
forgot the meeting of this Day of yours. Your refuge is the
Fire. You have no helpers. That is because you made a
mockery of Allah's signs and the life of the lower world
deluded you.' Therefore, today they will not get out of it.
They will not be able to placate Allah."*

(45:34-5)

It is narrated of Abu Hurayra that he said, "Whoever reaches
his sixtieth year, Allah will excuse him (for wrong actions) during
his life."[1] Ibn Battal says that this sixty years is a watershed as it
represents the age which comes after the great battles of life. It is a
time of turning to Allah and to a true feeling of fear before the
Divine. It is the moment when one is on the lookout for the
approaching meeting with one's destined end. Allah's excusing the
slave is a manifestation of His grace and kindness towards His
slaves in bringing them from a state of ignorance to one of knowledge. He excuses them and will not punish them unless there is
overwhelming proof against them, even if they have been exces-

---

1. The commentator on *Fayd al-Qadir* says that this is narrated by Ahmad in
his *Musnad* as reported by Ya'qub ibn 'Abd ar-Rahman from Abu Hazim from
Sa'id al-Maqbari from Abu Hurayra, and the compiler has indicated that it is a
good *hadith*; al-Bayhaqi also reported it with the same text from Abu Hurayra
and then adds that al-Bukhari uses it.

sive in their love of the *Dunya* and had excessive expectations of it – that is, as long as they have not wilfully disregarded the order to oppose their lower selves in the *Dunya*, as long as they have intended to obey what they were commanded to do and to restrain themselves from engaging in what was prohibited for them.

> In the *Sahih* of Muslim it is narrated from Harmala from Abu Hurayra: "The heart of an old man is like that of a young man in his love of two things: long life and wealth."

An-Nawawi says that the heart of an old man who is full of love of wealth is overcome by it in the same way as the vigour of a young man overcomes his youth.

> Abu 'Ubayda arrived with some goods from Bahrain and the Ansar heard of his arrival. They prayed the morning prayer together with the Messenger of Allah, may the peace and blessings of Allah be upon him, and then as he was leaving they approached him. The Messenger of Allah, may the peace and blessings of Allah be upon him, smiled when he saw them and said, "I believe you have heard that Abu 'Ubayda has arrived and that he has come with something?" They said, "Yes, O Messenger of Allah". He said, "Rejoice and have high hopes for what will make you happy for, by Allah, poverty is not the thing I fear most for you but rather I fear that the *Dunya* will become abundant for you as it became abundant for those before you and they vied with each other for it as you vie with each other and it distracted them as it distracts you".[1]

The word "vying" refers to a desire for something, a wish to have exclusive access and use of it. The root of this word in Arabic (*munafasa*) is from the word *nafis* meaning "something of value", that is, something sought after by those who value it.

Ibn Battal says that anyone for whom the flower of the *Dunya* has opened must be wary of the inevitable consequences of heedlessness associated with his being immersed in this beauty. He

---

1. *Fath al-Bari*, vol. 11, p. 247.

must be aware of the trials and difficulties associated with this heedlessness. One should thus beware of feeling safe from the deceptive outward allure of this world and one should not vie with others over the *Dunya*.

> Abu Hurayra narrates that the Messenger of Allah said, may the peace and blessings of Allah be upon him: "Two rapacious and hungry wolves who pass the night in a sheep pen when the owner is unaware of them and who kill and eat their prey are not more destructive than the love of wealth and rank in relation to the *deen* of a Muslim man"[1]

Wealth and rank are like two wolves which tear the *deen* of the believer to pieces, which corrupt it and devour his faith. Just as the two rapacious wolves represent the greatest of dangers for the sheep, so covetousness for wealth and rank represent the greatest of dangers for the believer. It is thus in the process of acquiring wealth that man loses many of his virtues.

Truthfulness, for instance, is not compatible with accumulating wealth. One is forced to tell lies to such an extent that it becomes a habit. Cheating is also frequently practised in the interest of greater profits but through it man loses many aspects of sincerity and integrity and also his awareness of Allah, may He be exalted. Miserliness with wealth is another result of man's love for it. It drives him to miserliness and stinginess so that he becomes mean with himself and his family and lax concerning the rights of Allah with the result that he refuses to pay *zakat* or at least grows negligent about it.[2]

1. According to al-Bayhaqi at-Tabarani relates this in *al-Awsat* and its chain of narration is good. It also occurs in the narration of Tirmidhi above.

2. The incident concerning Tha'lab ibn Hatib is famous when Tha'lab asked the Messenger, may the peace and blessings of Allah be on him, to make a supplication for him to become rich. When his wealth multiplied he became so mean and miserly regarding *zakat* that the Messenger, may the peace and blessings of Allah be upon him, refused it from him, just as Abu Bakr and 'Umar refused it of him. It was about Tha'lab that the following *ayat* was revealed: "*There are among them those who make a promise to Allah that 'if He were to give us of His abundance we would surely pay the* zakat *on it.'*"

As for love of rank and position, this is even more dangerous and more serious as it arises from the needs and aspirations of the lower self. It impels people to show off and chase after reputation and in so doing they lose all sincerity and their actions are brought to nothing.

All this distances a man from certainty in matters of faith and belief. It causes him to undertake his actions for the sake of this world alone, to forget the Next World, to abandon the rights of Allah and to commit all sorts of terrible crimes.

> *"When you said, 'Musa, we will not put up with just one kind of food, so ask your Lord to produce for us some of what the earth supplies: its green vegetables, cucumbers, grains, lentils and onions.' He said, 'Do you want to replace what is better with what is inferior? Go back to Egypt, then you will certainly have what you demand.' Abasement and destitution were stamped upon them. They brought down anger from Allah upon themselves. That happened because they rejected the signs of Allah and killed the Prophets without any legal right. That happened because they rebelled and went beyond the limits."*
>
> (2:60)

Allah had provided the tribe of Israel with manna and quails (and whatever Allah provides is necessarily good and wholesome) but they rejected that provision and said: "We will not put up with just one kind of food." They desired instead green vegetables, cucumbers, grains, lentils and onions and so preferred what was inferior to what was better and gave up the better thing. But what was the result? The result was their return to Egypt and having abasement and destitution stamped on them all for having submitted to the appetites of their stomachs rather than accepting what Allah provided. The incident took its course until they brought the anger of Allah upon them.

The children of Israel's rejection of what Allah provided was also in effect a rejection of the Messengers of Allah. Their faith was connected to what happened. When they belittled the blessings of Allah and rejected Allah's choice for them they were in effect belittling the prophetic Message directed to them. What followed happened because they rebelled against the Messengers of Allah and killed them.

"No indeed! We have given these people enjoyment, as We did their fathers, until life seems long and good to them. Do they not see how We come to the land, eroding it from its extremities. Or are they the victors?" (21:44)

This long, inherited enjoyment corrupts people's *fitra*: that is, their natural form of behaviour. Enjoyment is a luxury and luxury corrupts the heart and stupefies the senses, which in turn ends in weakening of faith in Allah, dulling of insight and incapacity to reflect upon His *ayats*. So this is a trial and a testing by means of Allah's blessings for people who have not awakened to the dangers of their own lower selves, who have not kept watch over them and who have not connected them constantly to Allah. Do not forget this!

Then Allah presents them with a phenomenon which occurs every day somewhere on the face of the earth: land erosion. This is a metaphor for what happens when small, aggressive states swallow up outlying portions of large empires until they shrink to petty kingdoms after having been great empires rich in resources and wealth. The lesson to be drawn from this is that Allah is capable of changing any situation to its opposite little by little, almost without those concerned being aware of it.[1]

It is narrated of 'Uqba ibn Amir al-Juhani that the Messenger of Allah, may the peace and blessings of Allah be upon him, said: "If you see Allah giving to a man whose whole way of life is based on disobedience then (know) that this is Allah's way of tempting him towards destruction." Then he recited the following *ayat* as proof: *"When they forgot what they had been reminded of, We opened up for them the doors to everything until, when they were exulting in what they had been given, We sud-*

1. Sayyid Qutb, *The Shade of the Qur'an*, p. 2381

72

*denly seized them and at once they were in despair. So the
last remnant of the people who did wrong was rooted out.
Praise belongs to Allah, the Lord of all the worlds!"*
(6:45-6)

How dangerous is this trial on earth! How difficult it is for man
to realise the reality of this trial, especially if it comes in the form
of blessings! The *hadith* gives some important indications that
everyone would do well not to forget, especially believers. One is
the fact that if blessings increase for somebody who perseveres in
disobedient behaviour, this is in reality an invitation to destruction,
a trap for the disobedient person, a strategem against him. His
unawareness of what awaits him only increases, his exultation
only intensifies, on account of the increasing number of things in
his possession.

The *ayat* is a warning to such people. *"When they forgot what
they had been reminded of, We opened up for them the doors to
everything..."* – when this happens their exultation increases and
while they exult they are heedless and they are seized suddenly,
unawares. This noble *ayat* conveys a clear picture to anyone who
is awake and aware. If something does happen and a calamity does
occur, such a person will recall that the cause has been made plain
and that no one will be excused.

It is narrated from Qatada ibn Nu'man ibn Zayd that the
Messenger of Allah, may the peace and blessings of Allah
be upon him, said, "Jibril revealed to me the best *sura* he
had revealed to me up to this point, saying: 'Peace Himself sends you greetings of peace, O Muhammad, and
says: "Surely I have inspired the *Dunya* to be resistant,
sparing, constrained and harsh with the *awliya'*, so that
they may look forward to their meeting with Me, and to be
expansive, easy and good for My enemies, so that they
will hate the prospect of their meeting with Me. Surely I
have made it a prison for My friends and a Paradise for
My enemies.'"[1]

---

1. Al-Bayhaqi says that this is narrated by at-Tabarani and the chain of transmission contains someone who is unknown.

The believer always experiences the bitterness of the *Dunya*. He is responsible for what happens in his life in this world and he fears the Reckoning but nevertheless knows that he is required to act. He fears that he will fall short of what is required of him when he remembers the terror of the grave and the separation of the life-force from his body. When he remembers the blowing of the Trumpet on the Last Day he cries: "How can anyone be exultant when he realises that there are two guardian angels appointed over him? How can life possibly be ease and joy for him when he knows for certain that the Angel of Death is at his door and is preparing to enter without first asking permission?"

The believer senses the greatness and vastness of Allah and realises his own incapacity. He perceives the blessings of Allah which have been bestowed on him and experiences shame at his inability to give sufficient thanks for them. This world is narrow and harsh and a prison for the believer whereas it is easy, good and expansive for the disbeliever. For the disbeliever it is his Paradise. The believer looks forward to the approaching meeting with Allah but the disbeliever feels only loathing.

> It is narrated from Fadala ibn 'Ubayd that the Messenger of Allah, may the peace and blessings of Allah be upon him, said: "O Allah, if anyone believes in You and bears witness that I am your Messenger, make him look forward to the meeting with You, make Your judgement of him easy and diminish the *Dunya* for him. If anyone does not believe in You and does not bear witness that I am Your Messenger, then do not make him look forward to the meeting with You and do not make Your judgement of him easy but increase the *Dunya* for him."

This *hadith* is related to the concern shown by the Messenger of Allah for the believers as described in the Qur'an where Allah, may He be exalted, says: *"Your suffering is distressful to him. He is deeply concerned for you, gentle and merciful to the believers."* (9:128) This supplication for the believers is a mercy for them and a proof of his concern for them. The Messenger, may the peace and blessings of Allah be upon him, makes this supplication for all who trust and believe in Allah and who affirm the Message – that a person's meeting with Allah may be something he looks forward to, that the judgement may be easy for him, that he will accept it in good spirit, that his portion of the *Dunya* may be small and that of the Next World greater. In the case of the disbeliever the opposite is true. His supplication is that he may not look forward to the meeting with Allah, that he may be constricted by the final judgement, that he may have a large portion of the *Dunya* but none of the Next World.

Abu'sh-Shaykh ibn Hibban narrates in *Kitab ath-Thawab* from Ibn 'Umar, may Allah be pleased with him and his father, that the latter said, "We went out with the Messenger of Allah, may the peace and blessings of Allah be upon him, and he entered some walled gardens belonging to the Ansar, where he began to pick up some dates from the ground and eat them. Then he asked me: 'Son of 'Umar, why are you not eating?' I said, 'I have no appetite for them, Messenger of Allah!' He replied, 'But I do have an appetite for them. This is the fourth morning that I have not tasted food. If I wished I could call upon my Lord, may He be be glorified, to give me as much as Chosroes and Caesar. How would you feel, son of 'Umar, if you were to stay with a people who put away provision for the year but whose certainty of belief became weakened?' By Allah we did not leave that place until the *ayat 'There is not a beast which does not bear its own provision with it. Allah provides for it and for you as well; and He is the All-Hearing, All-Knowing'* (29:60) was revealed. Then the Messenger of Allah said, may the peace and blessings of Allah be upon him: 'Surely Allah has not commanded me to store up the *Dunya* or to follow my desires. Anyone who stores up the *Dunya* wanting to have a permanence in it should know that life is in the Hand of Allah, may He be glorified. I do not store up even a *dinar* or a *dirham* and I do not put provision away even for the next day.'"[1]

1. This is narrated in *al-Taghrib*, vol. 5, p.149 and the like is related by Ibn

Prophethood and the perfect worship of Allah, the One, demonstrated by it is higher than all other ways of life and is the highest example for the generations that follow. Allah provided His Messenger Muhammad with what was sufficient, but ways and means were not automatically subjugated to him. His needs and necessities of life were not always automatically fulfilled. His Companions saw how he would fast from one day to the next. They wanted to imitate him but he forbade them to fast continuously in this way. When they said to him, "You fast one day after another," he explained to them that this matter was one of the privileges of Prophethood and an achievement which surpassed normal practice: "My being is not like that of any one of you. I pass the night with my Lord, Who feeds me and gives me to drink." This practice therefore had a prophetic form to it and was distinct from the normal human practice.

It may further be noted, with respect to this aspect of Prophethood, that the Messenger of Allah, may the peace and blessings of Allah be upon him, went for four days without tasting any food. Would it have been difficult, one may ask, for him to have entered these gardens of the Ansar during any one of the four days? No, it was simply a matter of a prophetic lesson which demonstrated how the normal pattern of behaviour could be broken and then taken up again once more later, an example which would resonate in man's ears until the Day of Resurrection. This prophetic lesson teaches mankind about the degree of certainty of the Prophet.

The elements of this prophetic teaching were as follows. For four days the Prophet did not taste any food. This was not through any lack of means on his part, for he could have called on his Lord, may He be glorified, to give him as much provision as Chosroes and Caesar. The Messenger of Allah comprehended the Unseen by means of what Allah had taught him, and by way of the gates of abundance that He had opened for him, so he asked Ibn 'Umar, "How would you feel, son of 'Umar, if you were to stay with a people who put away provision for the year?" So reflect, O

Abi Hatim from Ibn 'Umar. The chain of narration includes Abu al-'Atuf al-Jazari, and it is treated as a weak *hadith* in the Commentary of Ibn Kathir, vol. 3, p. 42.

brother Muslim, on those who have enough for a whole year. They store up grains or they have savings in the bank. Does this result in their feeling reassured or do their anxiety, care and grief increase as a result? The Messenger of Allah does not leave us in any confusion, rather he removes all doubt when he tells us that in fact the certainty of their belief is weakened.

This then is what we learn from those who cling to the *Dunya* and who fear that their bank balances will depreciate. Their covetousness increases, as does their miserliness and their anxiety about life. The prophetic image closes with an *ayat* which is intended to strengthen the link between the believer and his Lord and to increase his certainty so that he will not fear for his provision since this has been guaranteed by Allah. *"There is not a beast which does not bear its own provision with it. Allah provides for it and for you as well."* (29:60)

> It is narrated from Ibn 'Umar (in a chain of relation that does not lead directly back to him): "The health and safety of the first of this *Umma* came from their detachment and their certainty; and the destruction of the last of it will be by their miserliness and over-expectation."[1]

It is said that restraining one's expectations is the very essence of detachment although in fact it is its cause. Over-expectation generates laziness regarding acts of obedience (to Allah and His Messenger) and delay in turning to Him in repentance. It also generates desire for this world, causes one to forget the Next World, and hardens the heart. Submission and purity of the heart only come about through remembrance of death, of the grave, of the reward and the punishment, and of the states of the Day of Reckoning. Allah, may He be exalted, says: *"The time seemed too long for them and their hearts became hard."* (57:15) It is also said that exercising restraint in one's hopes can be achieved by a reduction in one's striving after this world and by the illumination of the heart. If a person brings death to mind he will naturally

---

1. This is narrated by at-Tabarani and Ibn Abi Dunya.

strive to perform acts of obedience, his endeavour in this world will be reduced and he will be content with a little.[1]

The manifestations of love of the *Dunya* and its consequences

It is narrated from 'Abdullah ibn 'Amr that the Prophet, may the peace and blessings of Allah be upon him, said: "There was a kid amongst a lot of other goats. It was suckled by its mother and its thirst was quenched. Then she had extra milk and suckled all the goats but the kid did not have its fill." Someone said that this is the likeness of a people who will come after you among whom is a man who is given sufficient for a whole tribe or a nation but then does not have his fill himself.[2]

This is an extraordinary parable. It explains the difference between holding to true values and faith – in the form of the *Shari'a* and its directives – and abandoning them in favour of this life and its pleasures and luxuries. Those who protect themselves by living according to the *Shari'a* will be content with what they are given and will discover love for others and solicitude for the community. They will take care to see to the needs of others. The kid, one goat among many, had enough to drink from its mother, who would suckle it and quench its thirst. But when its mother had extra milk and suckled all the other goats it did not get enough.

The *hadith* is sealed by an explanation of the meaning behind this parable: that a people will come afterwards, one of whom will be given enough for a whole tribe or nation and yet not have his fill. How many a man have we seen in poverty, for whom even a loaf of bread is enough to stem his hunger! But people who possess millions and reside in palaces whose furnishings alone cost millions are never satiated, because they are continually pursuing luxury, pursuing their desire for the pleasures of this life.

1. Ibn Hajar, *Fath al-Bari*, vol. 11, p. 241.
2. According to al-Haythami al-Bazzar and at-Tabarani, in *al-Awsat,* narrate this and the men of the chain of narration are trustworthy except 'Ata' ibn as-Sa'ib who grew confused (in his memory) before his death.

It is narrated from 'Abdullah ibn Mas'ud that the Messenger of Allah, may the peace and blessings of Allah be upon him, said: "Whoever becomes steeped in the love of this world, three things will cling to him: difficulty and troubles which will never cease; covetousness which will never be satisfied; and hope which will never be realised. The *Dunya* seeks and is sought after. If anyone seeks this world the Next World will seek him out until death comes to him and takes him; and if anyone seeks the Next World this world will seek him until he has his fill of provision from it."[1]

Love of this world, reliance on it and contentment with it are all causes of calamities and crises. Love of this world and a strong attachment to it bring about a swift end for the person concerned. The end, the punishment, is contained in the very essence of this love. It is this love which draws down upon him disasters and difficulties. Reflect upon the punishment which comes about in this world. The *hadith* warns every believer against becoming too attached to the *Dunya*.

"Difficulties and troubles which will never cease" are what first strike those who love this world and are attached to it. They become alienated from happiness and tranquillity, and difficulties and troubles take their place. This is not a temporary difficulty but an endless series of troubles. How can anyone find rest when they are enamoured of the world? No sooner does he obtain anything of benefit in it than he is overcome by anxiety about the threat of damage or loss to the thing he has obtained. He tries to get happiness, mastery and rank for himself, but what a vast difference there is between this imaginary happiness in this world and the promised happiness in the blessed Gardens of the Next World!

The happiness of this world is in direct proportion to what an individual aspires to but that of the Next World is in proportion to the esteem the believer is held in by Allah, may He be exalted. The capacity and capability of an individual is extremely limited. He may try and strive but inevitably fails to achieve everything he

---

1. Narrated by at-Tabarani and classed as trustworthy by al-Haythami.

desires. The result of this discrepancy is that he feels wretchedness, dejectedness, failure. It is this state which causes difficulties and troubles which never cease. And even if a man does obtain some good and blessing for himself in the *Dunya*, however insubstantial, he often lives in fear and covetousness. He fears that the blessing will come to an end or will be removed from him. He becomes greedy for its continuance and is tormented by confusion, anxiety and heedlessness – all of which will inevitably bring loss.

At this point we come to another characteristic which the Prophet, may the peace and blessings of Allah be upon him, mentioned above: "covetousness which will never be satisfied". This covetousnoess manifests as a constant greed for the *Dunya* but this will be of no use to him as what is in the *Dunya,* or indeed the *Dunya* itself, can disappear at any moment.

As for his words "hope which will never be realised", this indicates a person who is always in a state of wanting and searching. Every time something is fulfilled for him, he hopes for something else and so he is in a constant state of distraction. Allah, may He be exalted, says as a warning and admonition: *"Leave them to eat and enjoy themselves. Let false hope divert them. They will soon know."* (15:3)

The *hadith* continues with a description of the state of the people who seek after this world, who love it and live for it. They are depicted as owing something to the Next World. It is as if the Next World were standing at their door demanding that they pay what they owe – right up to the moment when death comes and they are unable to pay anything they owe for the Next World and so perish and become losers.

The state of those who perform their actions for the Next World is very different. People whose concern is for the Next World, who are occupied with the affairs of the Next World – such people live like lords. They are served by Existence and the *Dunya* stands at their door as a servant, obedient to them, so that they obtain everything they need from it.

It is narrated from 'Abdullah ibn Mas'ud that the Messenger of Allah said, may the peace and blessings of Allah be upon him: "Do not acquire landed property and so become desirers of the *Dunya*."[1]

Surely the possession of estates and palaces causes man to become attached to the *Dunya*, to desire it. It is only faith which saves man from this. Consider what the believer said to his colleague, the owner of the two gardens: *"Why, when you entered your garden, did you not say, 'As Allah wills, there is no strength but in Allah'?"* (18:38) The *hadith* warns the believer against taking lands and property as all his aspirations and endeavour would then become directed towards it, and all his concern and love would be for it. As a result his attachment to the Next World would weaken, as would his concern for and contentment with it.

Abu Nu'aym narrates in *al-Hilya* that 'A'isha, may Allah be pleased with her, said, "Once I put on a new dress of mine and began to look at it and become captivated by it. Then Abu Bakr, may Allah be pleased with him, said, 'What are you looking at? Surely Allah is not looking at you.' I replied, 'Why not?' He said, 'Do you not realise that when someone becomes captivated by the beauty of this world Allah, may He be exalted, hates him until he separates himself from this beauty?'" She added, "So I took it off and gave it away." Abu Bakr then observed: "It may be that this action will make amends (for previous wrong actions)."[2]

This is a voice from the past which is still resonating in our ears. Reflect upon this scene in all its vital immediacy. The Mother of the Believers, 'A'isha, may Allah be pleased with her, puts on a new dress. She becomes fascinated by it and starts to look at it and feel proud of it. Then Abu Bakr, may Allah be pleased with him, realises what is going on. He puts the matter right by showing her the reality of the situation. He asks what she is looking at, putting the value of the dress and its beauty into perspective. Certainly it will wear out and eventually disintegrate. Abu Bakr then says that

1. According to at-Tirmidhi this is a good *hadith*.
2. *Hilyat al-Awliya'*, vol. 1, p. 37.

81

Allah is not looking at her. Why is that? She is not committing an obvious wrong action. Abu Bakr is simply indicating to her the trial and difficulties which are inherent in the beauty of the life of this world. 'A'isha is a Mother of the Believers and it is well known that the good actions of the righteous count as wrong actions for those who have been brought close to Allah. Abu Bakr as-Siddiq points out the truth and reality underlying her situation or rather he reminds her of it.

When admiration and vanity, which are based on the beauty of this world, enter a person's heart, then his Lord hates him until he separates himself from this beauty. How can the slave extricate himself from the beauty of this world? The answer was given by 'A'isha, may Allah be pleased with her, when she gave away the dress she had become so fascinated with. It is as if it were a lesson drawn from experience which the Mother of the Believers gave for the generations to come. She is calling on them to free themselves from fascination with the beauty of this world.

> *"We have tried them as We tried the owners of the garden when they swore that they would harvest in the morning but did not say the redeeming words, 'If Allah wills'. So a visitation from your Lord came to it while they slept and in the morning it was like burnt land stripped bare. In the morning they called out to one another, 'Leave early for your land if you are going to pick.' So they set off, quietly telling one another, 'Do not let any poor man into it today while you are there.' They left early, intent on carrying out their scheme. But when they saw it, they said, 'We have missed our way. No, the truth is that we are destitute.' The best of them said, 'Did I not say to you, "Why do you not glorify Allah?"' They said, 'Glory be to our Lord. Truly we have been wrongdoers.' They turned to face each other in mutual blame. They said, 'Woe to us! We were indeed exorbitant. Maybe our Lord will give us something better than it instead. We make entreaty to our Lord .' Such is the punishment; and the punishment of the Next World is much greater if they but knew."* (68:17-33)

This story explains the nature of injustice and oppression. Reflect upon the scene, reflect upon the owners of gardens at harvest time! Some people are intent on going to orchards to glean some of the fruit. They are destitute and in need of this fruit. We are told that one of the owners of the gardens used to set aside a portion for the poor but that when the man died his garden was inherited by his children and they considered that what their father used to give to the poor was too much. They coveted all the fruit and so they came to a decision amongst themselves. What arbitrary and reckless behaviour there is in the decisions of the greedy! The beginning of the decision was an oath: "and they swore...".

That decision then becomes a contract which these covetous persons make together, binding themselves to it by this oath. After the oath comes their intent: "that they would harvest in the morning" – that is, that they would pick the fruit before any of the destitute arrive. Then comes the conclusion of their decision: "but did not say the redeeming words, 'If Allah wills' – or as some commentators interpret: "but did not reserve a portion of the fruit for the poor and the destitute."

The divine response comes immediately – "while they slept": that is, a storm came and wrought havoc. The fruit was ruined and it was as if it had already been gathered. Then they woke up. Reflect upon the state of heedlessness they were enveloped in. They called upon each other early in the morning and urged each other on so that they might achieve their aim. They left whispering to each other, as if reminding each other of their agreement: "Do not let any poor man into it today while you are there."

They were afraid to raise their voices in case they woke up some of the poor and needy, so much had their greed and egoism corrupted them. Then we read: "They left early, intent on carrying out their scheme". At this point their state indicates they were full of confidence and certain of obtaining the fruit of the gardens, full of greedy expectation for what was awaiting them. But their confidence and self-delusion disintegrates into incapacity and loss: "But when they saw it..." in its new and strange state, its fruit destroyed and the trellises collapsed, they at first refuse to believe their eyes and say: "We have missed our way." But then they realise the full import of what has happened.

It is they who are now destitute. How difficult it is for those who experience destitution after their desire has been inflamed for fruits, harvest and wealth! It is as if the hand of Divine Power has banished those people who left early in the morning, has reduced them to join the ranks of the needy – those whom they themselves had wished to deprive – so as to make them taste the bitterness of deprivation. He has done so in order to teach them the excellence of giving so that it may be a lesson for those willing to learn the lesson.

Then we read that the best of them said "Did I not say to you: 'Why do you not glorify Allah?'" when he realised the devastation. It is as if the answer to the blight and desolation came after they witnessed the shock of loss of the harvest and they started to blame each other. "They turned to face each other in mutual blame." There was no rightly guided person amongst them who was able to advise and direct them. This area of blight became a zone of manifest transgression and opression and so their lament was: "Woe to us! We were indeed exorbitant." In this story there are certainly signs for those who are able to be reminded.

> *"We sent Messengers to nations before you, and seized them with poverty and illness so that perhaps they might humble themselves. If only they had humbled themselves when Our violent force came upon them! But their hearts were hard and Shaytan made what they were doing seem good to them. When they forgot what they had been reminded of, We opened up for them the doors to every-thing until, when they were exulting in what they had been given, We suddenly seized them and at once they were in despair. So the last remnant of the people who did wrong was rooted out. Praise belongs to Allah, the Lord of all the worlds!" (6:43-46)*

Reflect upon this luring into temptation and upon the stages in which it comes about. Allah opens the door of humility and fear of

Allah for them. It is through this door that it is fitting for the slave to go to his Lord. How else should a slave enter upon his Lord and be accepted if not by the door of lowliness?

So reflect upon how the matter is expressed in the Qur'an. It is as if there is regret for those who refuse to enter upon their Lord by the door of humility, fear of Allah and submission. "If only they had humbled themselves when Our violent force came upon them!" This is an unusual expression which indicates the extent of the loss suffered by these fractious people. But the hardness of their hearts becomes manifest and they do not respond to the possibility of submission they have been offered. "But their hearts were hard."

All feelings of good are stifled, and their antipathy and recalcitrance increase. Shaytan makes the whole thing appear fine to them and tricks them. They forget the reminder they received and the harsh reality of enticement and allurement follows. "When they forgot what they had been reminded of, We opened up for them the doors to everything." But they treat this with contempt and submerge themselves in what they imagine is good and of benefit to them. In fact what they have been given is merely access to a door of redoubled torment.

Their complacency increases as they set about enjoying the ease they have been allowed and their increase in wealth. New houses are built and and there is an atmosphere of festivity and celebration. "...until, when they were exulting in what they had been given", that is, when they were at the height of their exuberance, they were suddenly overwhelmed by calamity and disaster. "We suddenly seized them." Then they are overcome with pain at the intensity of the attack: "...and at once they were in despair," – that is, despairing of the mercy of Allah, may He be exalted. And so they can be seen broken and dejected.

Do you realise now how their state and condition has been changed? How they have lost their way? How their happiness and joy has been transformed into hopelessness, dejection, brokenness and despair? Then Allah concludes with the words: *"So the last remnant of the people who did wrong was rooted out. Praise belongs to Allah, the Lord of all the worlds!"*

When Allah says: "When they forgot what they had been reminded of," He means that they spurned Him and turned their backs on Him. When He says: "We opened up for them the doors to everything", He means that He opened up for them the doors of provision so that anything they wanted was theirs for the choosing. But that is only a trial and an enticement from Allah and for this reason He says, "...until, when they were exulting in what they had been given" - that is, by way of wealth, of children and provision - "We suddenly seized them", that is when they were heedless and unaware.

The words "and at once they were in despair" refers to their despair at all the good things they had lost. Hasan al-Basri said: "Those to whom Allah gives abundant provision but who do not realise that they are being enticed into a trap have no faculty of judgement. Those who find their means of livelihood have been straitened but do not see that that is a sign of kind attention from Allah also lack judgement."

Ibn Abi Hatim narrated from 'Ubada ibn al-Samit that the Messenger of Allah said, may the peace and blessings of Allah be upon him: "If Allah wants continuation and growth for a people, He bestows frugality and modesty on them; but if Allah wants a people to be cut off, He opens the stores of provision up for them." In other words, He opens up the door of deception to them just as He says in the words: "...until, when they were exulting in what they had been given, We suddenly seized them and at once they were in despair." Allah, may He be exalted, describes the result as follows: *"So the last remnant of the people who did wrong was rooted out. Praise belongs to Allah, the Lord of all the worlds!"* [1]

Ahmad narrated with his chain of narration from 'Uqba ibn 'Amir from the Prophet, may the peace and blessings of Allah be upon him, that he said: "When you see Allah giving a slave whatever of the *Dunya* he wants, despite his disobedience, then know that this is a trial." And then the Messenger of Allah recited: *"When they forgot what they had been reminded of, We opened up for them the doors to everything until, when they were exulting in what they had been given, We suddenly seized them and at once*

---

1. Ibn Kathir, *Tafsir*, vol. 1, p. 143: he says that Ahmad and others narrated it.

86

*they were in despair. So the last remnant of the people who did
wrong was rooted out. Praise belongs to Allah, the Lord of all the
worlds!"*

> *"Whoever desires the life of this world and its finery, We
> will give them full payment in it for their actions. They
> will not be deprived of their due in it. Such people shall
> have nothing in the Next World but the Fire. What they
> achieved in it will come to nothing. What they did will
> prove null and void."* (11:15-16)

The product of any striving on this earth, whether the person
concerned has his sights on the highest of ambitions or on something of immediate material benefit, is, in its essence, limited.
Whoever wants the life of this world and its adornment and acts
for that alone will receive any benefit accruing from his actions in
the *Dunya* and will be able to enjoy the fruit of those actions as he
wants – within the limited period of his term on this earth. But he
will have nothing in the Next World except the Fire since he will
have sent nothing forward to it. There will be nothing in the Balance there for him. He will be puffed up with the enjoyment, material pleasure and benefits of this world, which are hollow and
worthless in comparison with the Hereafter and which are doomed
to disappear.

We see that nowadays there are individuals, indeed whole peoples, tribes and nations, who work only for this world. They obtain
the reward of their actions during this life but that reward is a hollow, cancerous, inflated thing. We can hardly be expected to be
surprised at this state of affairs, for whatever happens to such people is part of the *Sunna* of Allah on this earth. Allah, may He be
exalted, says: *"As for any who desire the life of this world and its
finery, We will give them full payment in it for their actions. They
will not be deprived of their due in it."*

On the other hand, if people kept themselves directed towards
the Hereafter, keeping Allah in their sights, during their acquisition
of the material benefits of the *Dunya* and in their enjoyment of
pleasures, they would attain the beauty of the life of the *Dunya* and

would not be deprived of any of it while at the same time obtaining the pleasure of the life of the Next World. Actions undertaken for the sake of the life of the Next World are not necessarily outwardly different from actions undertaken for the sake of the life of this world. In fact sometimes the actions are exactly the same except for the fact that they are performed "for the Cause of Allah".

Awareness of Allah does not decrease in accordance with the number of actions undertaken in this world but rather increases. Indeed the striving and its reward are all the more blessed and render any gain or profit good and wholesome just as it does any pleasure or ease acquired through such actions. The problem comes when the pleasures of this world dominate and obscure the pleasures of the Next World, especially when the intention associated with the words "pleasures of this world" is that of forbidden passions – as the history of man down the ages bears witness.

Al-'Awfi narrates from Ibn 'Abbas concerning this *ayat* that even those who act for show are rewarded in accordance with their good actions in the world. This is because, as the Qur'an tells us, Allah does not treat anyone unjustly in any way. When such a person performs good actions, whether fasting, prayer or night devotions, but does them only seeking the *Dunya*, Allah will say, "Give him the reward he sought in this world, but make the action worthless because he only did it for the sake of the *Dunya;* and cause him to be one of the losers in the Next World."

Qatada says, "If someone makes the *Dunya* the goal of his endeavour, intention and seeking, Allah will reward him for his good actions in it, but when he proceeds to the Next World, he will not have a single good action for which he will be rewarded."[1]

The necessities of life

It is narrated from Abu Hasana Muslim ibn Akyas, the client of 'Abdullah ibn 'Amir, that Abu 'Ubayda ibn al-Jarrah, may Allah be pleased with him, said someone entered his house and finding him weeping asked him:

1. Ibn Kathir, *Tafsir*, vol. 2, p. 471.

"What is making you weep, Abu 'Ubayda?" He replied, "We are weeping because the Messenger of Allah, may the peace and blessings of Allah be upon him, mentioned the day when Allah would open up the territories for the Muslims and bestow booty on them. He mentioned what would happened in Sham (Greater Syria) and then said, 'If long life is granted you, Abu Ubayda, then may three servants be enough for you: a servant to serve you, a servant to travel with you, and a servant to serve your family and to attend to them; and may three beasts be enough for you: a beast for your journey, a beast to carry your heavy things, and a beast for your servant boy.' But when I look at my house I find it filled with slaves and when I look at my stables and find them full of animals, so how am I to meet the Messenger of Allah, may the peace and blessings of Allah be upon him, after that? The Messenger of Allah, may the peace and blessings of Allah be upon him, then advised me, saying: 'The person most beloved to me and the nearest to me is the one who meets me in the same state in which he parted company from me.'"

So three servants are sufficient and three animals are sufficient. As for servants, it is enough to have one for service, another for journeys and a third to serve one's family. As for the animals, there should be one for travel, a second to carry loads and heavy articles and a third for one's servant. Things of the *Dunya* come easily to some people, however, and Abu 'Ubayda's material possessions increased so that he began to feel the weight of responsibility for them and exhausted by them. He also realised that any increase in the number of his beasts or increase in his wealth also meant an increase in the distance between him and his beloved Muhammad, may the peace and blessings of Allah be upon him. For the Messenger of Allah, may the peace and blessings of Allah be upon him, had advised him that those most loved by him and closest to him were the people who met him in the same state as the state they had been in when they last saw him.

This represents one aspect of fulfilling one's contract or agreement with others, one aspect of the respect which is the right of companionship. What we may understand from this *hadith* is that man should only make use of the material things of life such as servants and mounts to the extent that he is he is able to afford them according to his real needs.

> It is narrated from al-Hasan that when Salman came one day he wept saying, "The Messenger of Allah, may the peace and blessings of Allah be upon him, told us that the amount we were to acquire of the *Dunya* should be no more than what is equal to the provision of a rider, but we have abandoned that commitment." When they examined what he (Salman) left, they found it to be worth no more than twenty or thirty dirhams.

> It is narrated from Burayda al-Aslami that the Messenger of Allah, may the peace and blessings of Allah be upon him, said: "Let a servant and a mount be enough of the world for any of you."[1]

When the Prophet, may the peace and blessings of Allah be upon him, commanded people to give *sadaqa*, the Companions hastened to do good actions and vied with each other to obey – even the poor who were themselves entitled to receive *sadaqa* from others. Because of the importance they attached to being Companions of the Messenger of Allah, they felt obliged to perform extraordinary actions. So it was that a poor man went out in response to the command of the Messenger of Allah, may the peace and blessings of Allah be upon him, and became a porter, carrying other people's things and transporting them for a small wage so that he could come with a measure of dates or grains and give it in *sadaqa*.

It may well be that the fortunes of the *Dunya* smile on some people and the flower of the *Dunya* blossoms for them so that they amass a million. However, the desire and concern of the

---

1. Narrated by Imam Ahmad in his *Musnad*.

Companions, may Allah be pleased with them and have mercy on them, was that their state should remain close to that of the Messenger of Allah, may the peace and blessings of Allah be upon him, so they felt a constant worry whenever their provision increased.

We see in the case of Salman, may Allah be pleased with him, that he began to weep when his wealth increased above the amount which the Messenger of Allah had stipulated. And what was it that Salman, may Allah be pleased with him, left? He left thirty odd dirhams, at the highest estimate! May Allah have mercy on you and be pleased with you, Salman, and with your Companions who truly understood the Messenger of Allah, may the peace and blessings of Allah be upon him. What they understood was that the basic necessities of life are sufficient as the Messenger of Allah, may the peace and blessings of Allah be upon him, told them. For anything more than that there is a reckoning which might go for you or against you.

> Ibn Abi'd-Dunya and al-Dinawari relate from Sufyan ibn 'Uyayna that he said: "Sa'd ibn Abi Waqqas wrote to 'Umar ibn al-Khattab, may Allah be pleased with them both, while he was in Kufa asking for permission to build a house to live in. He wrote back: 'Build what will simply shield you from the sun and shelter you from the rain, for surely this world is the abode in which what suffices is enough'"[1]

This is an echo from the past, an example and a teaching by which the governor seeks permission from the Amir to build a house to protect himself. Extravagant many-storeyed buildings are a sign of the imminent coming of the Last Day, an indication of the collapse of civilisation. For this reason it is not fitting for the believer to exceed the bounds of what is absolutely necessary, as 'Umar, may Allah be pleased with him, made abundantly clear. The words of Allah, may He be exalted, in *Surat ar-Rahman* come to mind in this context. *"He erected heaven and established the*

---

1. Quoted from *Muntakhab al-Kanz*, vol. 4, p. 406.

balance, so that you would not overstep in the balance. Give just weight; do not skimp in the balance." (55:5-7)

I have reflected upon what is meant by 'the balance"[1] in the various *ayats* and it appears to me, but Allah knows best, that its meaning on the first two occasions refers to the natural laws which govern life in general (like the law of gravity, etc. which keep existence in order and ensure its continuance) just as Allah, may He be exalted says, *"...and revealed, in every heaven, its ordinance."* (41:12) What is meant here by the word "ordinance" is the same as what is meant by the word "balance", though Allah knows best: that is, the natural laws. It is for this reason that Allah, may He be exalted, says, *"so that you would not overstep in the balance."* This is a prohibition against overstepping the bounds regarding scientific developments and technological inventions lest the natural balance in creation be disturbed – as has happened in so many areas of life.

The purpose of this digression is to emphasize the concern of Islam, in all its texts and directives, for moderation and balance in everything and its concern that there be no excess, waste or extravagance. Despite this teaching, man is still in the habit of striving towards the most excessive goals in his experiments, research and inventions. For hundreds of years man has been able to read the warning in the Qur'an where Allah says, may He be exalted: *"Corruption has appeared in the land and the sea because of what people's hands have wrought, so that they may taste something of what they have done."*

Muslims must understand, reflect upon, and act by the light of this wisdom. The directives given by 'Umar to his governors were by way of example. Muslims must understand the danger of waste and extravagance in building. The Messenger of Allah himself, may the peace and blessings of Allah be upon him, had alerted him to this. Indeed it is one of the signs of the Last Day and an indication of the collapse of civilisation.

It is narrated from 'Uthman ibn 'Affan that the Prophet, may the peace and blessings of Allah be upon him,

---

1. We have already discussed this subject but there is no harm in repeating the idea.

declared, "The son of Adam only has a right to three things: a house to live in, clothes to cover his nakedness and dry bread and water."[1]

These then are the bare necessities of life. It is by means of these things that a man's life can be established: a house, clothes, and food and drink. They are the foundations of life and they alone are all that we have an absolute right to. Anything beyond this is extra. This advice is a warning to those who would abandon themselves to the whims and desires of aquisitiveness and to the greed and covetousness of the lower self for wealth and the pleasures of existence.

Ahmad narrates from 'Abdullah ibn az-Zubayr: "I entered into the same room as 'Ali ibn Abi Talib, may Allah be pleased with him, on the Day of *Adha* and he brought us some rich rice broth. We said, 'May Allah fortify you for having given us this bowl of rice, for surely Allah's bounty is great.' He replied, 'O Ibn Zubayr, I heard the Messenger of Allah, may the peace and blessings of Allah be upon him, say, "The only wealth lawful for the Caliph is two large bowls: one bowl that he and his family eat from and one bowl which he sets down before his guests."'" It is narrated in this form in Ibn Kathir's *Bidayat an-Nihaya* (vol.8, p.3).[2]

There is no doubt that Allah's bounty is great, but governance is a great responsibility and the governor is responsible for the state of the Muslims and their wealth. He must not neglect their affairs or waste their wealth. No wealth is lawful for the governor, we are told, but that which he sets before his family and the amount they need to sustain themselves and that which he presents to his guests. The governor has a reckoning before Allah, may He be exalted, concerning that for which Allah has made him respon-

1. At-Tirmidhi describes this *hadith* as good and sound.
2. The use of the word *Khalifa* and applying it to *Amirs* is something which came into use after the time of revelation. This is perhaps an indication of the weakness of the *hadith*. Allah knows best.

sible. He is answerable for safeguarding it and is accountable for anything which he neglects or causes to be lost.

It is narrated from Yahya ibn Ja'da that some people from amongst the Companions of the Messenger, may the peace and blessings of Allah be upon him, came back trotting on horseback saying: "Rejoice, O Abu 'Abdullah! Come to Muhammad, may the peace and blessings of Allah be upon him." Then he said: "But how can I?"–and he pointed at the top and bottom floors of his house – "when the Messenger of Allah, may the peace and blessings of Allah be upon him, has enjoined upon us that the amount we were to acquire of the *Dunya* should be no more than what is equal to the provision carried by a mounted man?"[1]

So we understand that the condition for coming into the presence of the Messenger of Allah, may the peace and blessings of Allah be upon him, is that a person be in a state of detachment in the *Dunya* and be looking forward to the Next World. Looking ahead to the next world does not mean merely making supplications. Detachment must not merely be a matter of wishful thinking, for the Messenger of Allah, may the peace and blessings of Allah be upon him, said that the amount we were to acquire of the *Dunya* should be no more than the equivalent of the provision of a mounted man. This, then, is the state of the person who is serious about his seeking after the Next World, serious about his journeying to it.

It is narrated from Abu'd-Darda' that the Messenger of Allah said, may the peace and blessings of Allah be upon him: "Whoever wakes up in the morning with his body in good health, tranquil in his state of mind and in possession of his day's provision, it is as if he had acquired the world in its entirety. O son of Adam, a small plate of food should

---

1. This is narrated by Abu Ya'la and at-Tabarani, whose narraters are sound except Yahya ibn Ja'da – although he has the rank of trustworthiness according to al-Bayhaqi.

suffice you to satisfy your hunger and a cloth to cover your nakedness, and if there is a house which covers your nakedness then so be it, and if there is a beast then all the better. But a portion of bread and a jug of water is enough and anything more than a loin-cloth is a surplus for which you will be held accountable."

It is narrated from 'Umar that he said that the Messenger of Allah, may the peace and blessings of Allah be upon him, said, "Son of Adam, you have enough to satisfy you but you seek what will cause you to transgress. You are not made content by little and you do not get your fill from much. O son of Adam, if you awake in the morning, tranquil in your state of mind, with your body in a good state of health, in possession of provision for your day then your are freed from the *Dunya.*"

Abu Hurayra said that the Messenger of Allah, may the peace and blessings of Allah be upon him, said: "Desires and whims will eventually get to you, you who enjoy well-being and vitality."

I have thought a great deal about these blessed *hadiths*. We gulp down large draughts of the bounty of life, drawing from its springs and drinking from its sources of goodness. We control the natural laws: that is, we manipulate them to serve us over and above the natural restraints and bounds inherent in them so that there are now aeroplanes flying high in the skies, cars speeding along our roads, water coolers and air conditioners fulfilling the sweetest of our dreams, and machines and instruments for shipping, despatch and communication which make a constant din of activity – all of which we find both fascinating and alluring.

I have reflected upon how sufficiency and contentment in life is what is really to be desired. Life in this world can only be measured in terms of a person's concern for the means of subsistence, just as the life of the believer in the Next World can only be measured in terms of how easy the Reckoning is for him. The needs of life may be defined as a healthy body free of disease and pain, a

95

feeling of security and reassurance in society and in the family, and the availability of or the capacity to acquire a day's sustenance. This is the *Dunya*. So ponder the words of the Messenger, may the peace and blessings of Allah be upon him, and understand them, and act accordingly.

> 'Abdullah ibn 'Umar, may Allah be pleased with him and his father, said that the Messenger of Allah, may the peace and blessings of Allah be upon him, took me by the shoulders saying, "Be in this world as if you are a stranger or a traveller." And Ibn 'Umar would say, "When evening comes then do not expect the morning to arrive and when morning comes then do not expect the evening to arrive. Take from your health for your sickness and from your life for your death."[1]

Ibn Battal comments that a stranger is someone who has little to do with people, and indeed is alien to them. He hardly passes anyone whom he knows or he feels close to, with the result that he is humble and fearful. The same is true of the traveller. He can only reach the end of his journey by means of the provision he is carrying with him and by travelling light, unburdened by anything heavy or cumbersome such as would prevent him from completing the journey. He has with him only his provision and his mount and it is only by means of these two things that he is able to reach his destination. In this way too he is like the stranger, cut off from those amongst whom he is travelling. There is an indication in this that it is preferable to do without in this world and that one should just take sufficient for one to carry out what one has to do. Just as the traveller does not need anything beyond what will take him to his destination, so the believer does not need anything more in the *Dunya* beyond what will get him to the ultimate purpose and object of it: his death and the *Akhira*.

Someone else said that this *hadith* is clear proof of the need to separate oneself from the *Dunya*, to do without in it, to despise it and to be content with whatever one has.

---

1. See *Fath al-Bari*, p. 237 and following pages.

According to an-Nawawi the meaning of the *hadith* is that you should not rely on the *Dunya*; you should not take it as your permanent abode; you should not delude yourself that you are going to be in it forever; and you should not cling to it any more than a stranger would cling to somewhere which is not his home country.

Another scholar said that a traveller is a person who is moving homewards along a road. So a person in this world is like a slave sent by his master on a mission to a country which is not his. He must do what he has to do as quickly as possible, return to his country and not get caught up in anything which does not concern him.

It is also said that the reason why a believer should consider himself a stranger in this world is not only so that his heart does not get attached to anything in this alien place but also so that his heart may become attached to the abode towards which he is returning. Thus he makes his stay in this world a means of focusing on his return and uses it to acquire what he needs to facilitate his return.

Ibn 'Umar says that the Messenger of Allah, may the peace and blessings of Allah be upon him, took hold of him by part of his body saying: "Be in this world as if you are a stranger or a traveller and count yourself as one of the inhabitants of the grave."[1]

These are truths and realities which are obscured by any attachment to the world. It is up to the intelligent man to remember firstly that he is a stranger in this world and the real position of the stranger is that he is travelling in an alien land which is not his home and secondly that he is destined to be one of the inhabitants of the grave, that he will inevitably be one of its residents and that he may have to enter it at any moment without prior warning. There are countless examples of the way death strikes suddenly. If you truly understand these things then this world will be of no value to you. You will act in it as would a hired worker working for his wage. He builds and establishes things not to own or to rule but to take his salary, his reward. The believer is like a wage-earner who is in expectation of his wage from Allah, may He be exalted.

1. This is narrated by at-Tirmidhi with chains of narration that are well attested.

According to Bara' ibn 'Azib, the Messenger of Allah, may the peace and blessings of Allah be upon him, said: "Whoever gratifies his desires and appetites in this world will be prevented from fulfilling his desires in the Next World;[1] whoever stretches his gaze to the adornments of those living in luxury will be despised in the Realms of the Heavens; and whoever puts up with a difficult provision with patient forbearance Allah will give him a place in Paradise wherever he wishes."[2]

The Qur'an reproaches the disbelievers for spending their time in the pursuit of pleasures and for the way they eat like animals. Allah, may He be exalted, says that the Fire is their ultimate abode. They will be hurled into it on to their faces by their lusts and they will wander aimlessly about.

The believer should use his intellect and conduct himself with calmness and tranquillity. He should only take of the *Dunya* as much as he has been permitted to take by Allah, may He be exalted. If he carries on like a blind person satisfying his most outrageous passions and lusts and drinking from every source, it is inevitable that he will fall into the *haram* and *"that a barrier will be set up between them and what they desire"*. Whoever occupies his soul, his heart and mind with the beauty and adornment of the life of this world is exposing himself to disgrace because that is the thing that Allah despises most. But those who endure harshness of the *Dunya* with patient forbearance will have their place in the highest Paradise – wherever Allah wishes (or, indeed, perhaps wherever the slave wishes).

---

1. Allah, may He be exalted, says: *"You have caused your good things to go away in your worldly life... "* (46:20); A barrier will be set up between them and the thing that they desire, just as was done with their kind before. (34:54)

2. This is connected to the meaning contained in Allah's words, may He be exalted: *"Do not direct your eyes longingly to what We have given certain of them to enjoy, the flower of the life of this world, so that We can test them by it."* (20:130) The saying of the Messenger of Allah, may the peace and blessings of Allah be upon him, "with patient forbearance" means one without constriction or complaint but accompanied by contentment and submission. Its manifest proof comes when a Believer says at the time of crisis or disaster: 'Surely we belong to Allah and surely we are returning to Him.'

"Do not be deceived by the fact that the people who reject move freely about the earth. A brief enjoyment; then their shelter will be Hell. What an evil resting-place!"
(3:196-197)

The people who reject faith move freely about the earth; they take of it, they love it and they find pleasure in it. The believers can be deceived by what the disbeliever is granted. We have seen how many are blinded when they see Qarun in all his splendour. This prohibition *"Do not be deceived..."* is directed at the Prophet, may the peace and blessings of Allah be upon him, but is really a warning for all the Muslims and a reassurance for the Prophet, may the peace and blessings of Allah be upon him.

The moving about of the disbelievers is a general phenomenon in all countries. The believer, too, may be blessed by the means and capacity to move about freely and it may well be that Allah opens the treasures of this world to him as well. It may also be this would, however, that his provision is restricted. Whatever his situation, though, however constrained he may be, he is always blessed and he will be able, by Allah, to achieve his goals, lead a normal life, and enjoy his children and the company of his neighbours.

These small pleasures and blessings, however slight they may be, are in fact incomparably preferable to the torments of those who seem to enjoy unlimited blessings on this earth. Consider the abominable and terrible warning: "then their shelter will be Hell." This will be their abode and they will find no other shelter. This warning concludes with a bitter finality: "What an evil resting-place!" We seek refuge with Allah from such an end.

"Do not direct your eyes longingly to what We have given certain of them to enjoy, the flower of the life of this world, so that We can test them by it. Your Lord's provision is better and more lasting." (20:129-130)

The prohibition *"Do not direct your eyes longingly..."* is similar to the previous prohibition which commands man not to submit to the whims and fancies of the lower self – that is, not to become

99

deceived or envious of the things and places which the disbelievers have access to as they move freely about the land.

But reflect on this second prohibition. It concerns the perception of the senses and seeks to restrain the extent of the gaze. In effect this prohibition tries to limit the influence of the senses by means of restraints imposed by faith. The scrutiny of the gaze and the attentiveness of the ear are both actions which express the inclination of the heart and the attachment of the will to something.

When the *ayat* speaks of the eye not looking longingly, the prohibition of such scrutiny that it entails is in fact directed towards restraining man's attachment to this world. The form of the *Dunya* is like that of a flower. Its colours are beautiful and its smells are sweet but in fact the life of this world is ephemeral and its benefit little as its trophies are of no lasting value. That image of the life of this world as a flower is a clear indication of the test man faces. A flower may entice us by its perfume and colours and we may be enticed by our love of the short-lived flower away from the search for its everlasting fruit.

The conclusion which follows is full of generosity on the part of Allah, may He be exalted. *"Your Lord's provision is better and more lasting."* Allah begins by mentioning provision with all that this entails of ease and wealth, and all the happiness, repose and security which these things necessarily imply. He ends by mentioning that it will be those things which will truly last for ever.

> *"O you who believe! In your wives and your children there is an enemy for you so beware of them. And if you pardon and overlook and forgive, Allah is Ever-Forgiving, Most Merciful. Your wealth and your children are only a trial. But with Allah there is an enormous wage. So fear Allah as much as you are able to and listen and obey and spend well for yourselves. Those who are safeguarded from the greed of their own souls, such people are successful."* (64:14-16)

Ibn Zayd says that the words of Allah, may He be exalted, *"so beware of them..."*, mean "so far as your *deen* is concerned." Mujahid says that to misunderstand this would inevitably lead a man either to sever family relations or to disobey his Lord, and a man, despite his love for them, can but obey his Lord. Allah says *"Your wealth and your children are only a trial"*, that is, a test from Allah to determine which of His creatures will obey Him and which will disobey Him.

The Messenger of Allah, may the peace and blessings of Allah be upon him, was giving a talk one day when Hasan and Husayn, may Allah be pleased with them, came stumbling in, both wearing red shirts. The Messenger of Allah, may the peace and blessings of Allah be upon him, descended from the *minbar*, picked them up and set them down in front of him, saying, "Allah and His Messenger have spoken the truth. Your wealth and your children certainly are a test. I looked at these two children tripping up as they came in and was not able to wait but interrupted what I was saying to pick them up!" Abu Sa'id said reported the Messenger of Allah said, may the peace and blessings of Allah be upon him: "A child is the fruit of the heart but it is also what makes the heart cowardly for the child's sake, makes it avaricious and makes it want to hoard."

At-Tabarani narrates by a chain of narration from Abu Malik al-Ash'ari that the Messenger of Allah declared, may the peace and blessings of Allah be upon him: "Your enemy is not someone who, if you kill him, is the cause of your gaining victory or who, if he kills you, will cause you to enter the Garden. The one who may well be your enemy is the child who has come from your loins - then after that the greatest of enemies to you is that which your right hand possesses."[1]

---

1. Ibn Kathir, *Tafsir*, vol. 4, p. 399.

Chapter Five
Detachment in the *Dunya* is a Sign of Love of Allah

The meaning of 'detachment'

Detachment does not mean withdrawing from the life of this world or being in conflict with it. For the Lord has commanded His slaves, to action, saying, may His remembrance be honoured: *"Say: 'Act, for Allah will see your actions, and so will His Messenger and the believers."* (9:106) And after the clear call to the community to come to the Friday prayer there comes a further call to go out and be active in the world. *"Then when the prayer is finished disperse about the earth and seek Allah's favour; and remember Allah repeatedly so that perhaps you will be successful."* (62:10)

This action can be of various kinds, however, and has various stages. First comes the action itself and then the reward for the action. There is the energy one expends in seeing to one's daily needs. But there comes a moment when those needs are in fact no longer necessities and turn into extravagances or luxuries. This expenditure can become so excessive that it becomes pure waste and the person guilty of such wasteful expenditure himself borders on the criminal.

Strictly speaking, action undertaken out of necessity does not come under the heading of detachment: life cannot continue without it. The Messenger of Allah, may the peace and blessings of Allah be upon him, urged people to undertake manual work, saying: "No one eats better food than that which he has earned by the work of his own hands. The Prophet Da'ud used to eat from what he earned by the work of his own hands." Da'ud was a Prophet-King. It would have been possible for him to eat and spare himself and his body, since he certainly had the means.

Likewise, since obtaining a reward for an action does not normally imply any aspect of "detachment". The one who works must get the reward for the work he has carried out. If this were not the case, it would cause a breakdown in the way life functions and a breakdown of social relations. Moreoever, spending on the necessities of life is indispensable, as Allah, may He be exalted, says: *"And do not throw yourselves into destruction by your own hands."* (2:195) He says in another place: *"And do not kill yourselves."* (4:29) Anything more than this, however, implies an overstepping of what is necessary and what one needs.

On the other hand, the person who does without in the realm of action, that is, who desists from action, is contravening the fundamentals of rational behaviour and also contravening the body of knowledge transmitted to us from the Messenger, may the peace and blessings of Allah be upon him. Desisting from action is contrary to the laws of the *Shari'a* and it is the nearest thing to disobedience itself, just as refusing to take recompense for work which may be used to spend on the necessities of life is an act of disobedience.

As we have already seen in the noble *hadiths*, the Messenger, may the peace and blessings of Allah be upon him, used to command his Companions to give *sadaqa*. On one occasion one of them went off to do some portering work and came back with a measure of grains which he then gave away as *sadaqa*. On other occasions he would call people to action so that they could provide for themselves and their families and have something to give in *sadaqa*.

Those who do without luxury items or things which are not absolutely necessary possess the quality of the *salihun*, the right-acting, those who do not concern themselves with the pleasures of this world despite their capacity to obtain them. Just as doing without items of luxury is one of the marks of the *salihun*, waste and extravagance is a mark of those destined for destruction and remoteness from Allah, may He be exalted. He says: *"Surely He does not love the extravagant.*" (6:141) Let us now turn to some texts which deal with this matter.

'Umar, may Allah be pleased with him, said that the Messenger of Allah, may the peace and blessings of Allah be upon him, saw Mus'ab ibn 'Umayr, may Allah be pleased with him, coming towards him dressed in a goatskin which was wrapped around his middle and said: "Look at this man whose heart has been illuminated by Allah but who does not concern himself with this life or its extravagances. He has just finished seeing to the needs of his parents who nourished him with the best kind of food and drink. I saw him in previous days wearing a garment which he bought for two hundred dirhams but which out of love of Allah and love of His Messenger he has abandoned for what you see him wearing now."[1]

Thus in order to attend better to his duties towards Allah Mus'ab dressed in a goat-skin, unconcerned with the beauty of this world. He had been motivated towards this by his love of Allah and love of His Messenger to the extent that he abandoned his garment worth two hundred dirhams and was content to cover his nakedness with the very sparsest and coursest of material.

Abu'd-Darda', may Allah be pleased with him, said: "By the One who has the self of Abu'd-Darda' in his hand, I would not like to have a shop at the door of the mosque today, even if that meant I did not miss a single prayer or earned forty dinars each day and gave it as *sadaqa* for the Cause of Allah." Someone then asked: "Abu'd-Darda', what do you dislike about this?" He replied: "The severe trial of being called to account." In another narration it reads: "I would not be happy to stand in an alleyway at the door of the mosque buying and selling even if I were to get three hundred dinars and perform all the prayers in the mosque. I am not saying that Allah, may He be exalted,

---

1. Narrated by Tabarani, Bayhaqi, al-Hakim and Abu Nu'aym.

has not permitted selling and forbidden usury. It is because I would like to be among those 'who are not distracted by trade or selling from the remembrance of Allah.'"[1]

This, then, is another kind of warning about the guile and deceit of the *Dunya*. It is calling to an awareness which elevates one above the ephemeral pleasures of this world, despite the clearly defined parameters of sound and safe behaviour. Abu'd-Darda' did not wish to have a shop at the door of the mosque even though he would not miss a group prayer in the mosque and would be earning perhaps forty dinars (or three hundred according to the other narration) all of which he would spend for the Cause of Allah. When Abu'd-Darda' was asked what he disliked about all this he replied that he was not claiming that Allah, may He be exalted, had not permitted trade and forbidden usury but rather that he feared Allah's reckoning of him and did not wish to be among those distracted by trade or selling from the remembrance of Allah.

It is narrated from Muhammad ibn Ka'b that some people came as guests of Abu'd-Darda', may Allah be pleased with him, on a very cold night and he sent them some hot food but he did not sent them any blankets. One of them said, "He has sent some of us food but it is impossible for us to get through the night here in this cold unless I explain the situation to him." Another said, "Don't bother him." But the man disagreed and went to the door of the house and saw Abu'd-Darda' sitting there together with his wife who had nothing but undergarments on. The man then said, "I see that you have exactly the same covering that we are spending the night with." Abu'd-Darda then replied, "Surely we have a house to which we are moving to and we have sent our mattresses and bedding on to it. If we had anything of that sort we would have sent it to you. We have a difficult way before us, and he who travels light

---

1. This is narrated by Abu Nu'aym in *Hilyat al-Awliya'*, and by Abu 'Asakir.

is better off than he who is burdened. Do you understand what I am telling you?"[1]

Surely we have before us a clear example of a strong and determined will, a will which overcomes discomfort and overcomes difficult circumstances. Clearly he is a man who is looking to the future and has the expectation of generous Divine gifts. The echoes of prophethood still reverberate in the ears and heart of Abu'd-Darda'. His heart responds to these echoes and he remembers the saying of the Prophet: "Keep firm control of the ship, for surely the sea is deep; increase your provision, for surely the journey is long; lighten your load, for surely the way is difficult; and carry out actions correctly, for surely the one who scrutinises and examines is a person of insight."

"Do you understand what I am telling you?" Yes, Abu'd-Darda', we do understand! And we ask Allah that He be pleased with you, that He help us to imitate your example, and that He remove us from insurrections, trials and all evil.

It is narrated from Sa'da ibn Sa'd ibn Hudhayfa that Hudhayfa, may Allah be pleased with him, used to relate: "No day is more tranquil to my eye and more beloved to me than a day when I come to my family and I find they have no food and they say, 'We have not been able to come by either a little or a great amount.' This is because I heard the Messenger of Allah say, may the peace and blessings of Allah be upon him: 'Truly Allah is more protective of the believer in respect of the *Dunya* than the family of a sick person who prevent him from eating food; and Allah, may He be exalted, cares more for the believers in times of trial than the father is maintaining his child with all that is good.'"[2]

This world is not the abode of permanence or the abode of reward. The fact that the *Dunya* comes easily to some people but shrinks from others is not a sign that the person concerned is being

---

1. Ahmad narrates this and Ibn Jawzi also mentions it in *Sifa al-Safwa*.
2. Narrated by Abu Nu'aym and at-Tabarani.

either honoured or treated disparagingly. A believer is cared for by Allah in the same way a sick person is cared for by his family. If water is harmful to the invalid his family take care not to let him have it despite their strong love for him. Indeed their refusal to let him have it is a proof of their deep love for him. The believer is in the hands of Allah, the Most Merciful, the Ever- Forgiving. He maintains, nurtures and prepares him for the Abode of permanence, of continuance. For this reason He helps him to lessen his attachment to the abode of impermanence. So reflect, brother Muslim, on the state of the believer with his Lord. He is like a sick person being cared for by his family; like a child who is looked after in the best way by his father. Your Lord is always forgiving and full of mercy. The believer realises this and is not saddened by those things of the *Dunya* which have passed him by. He realises that this world is an abode from which one should take only the bare minimum: that is, enough for one's basic needs.

According to Rafi' ibn Khadij, the Messenger of Allah, may the peace and blessings of Allah be upon him, said: "If Allah, may He be exalted, loves someone, He protects him from the *Dunya* just as any of you might keep a sick person from drinking water for his own protection."[1]

The mercy of Allah, may He be exalted, is shown towards His slaves by His giving them only what is good for them. It may well be that the portion of the *Dunya* allotted to the disbelievers by Allah is houses with magnificent staircases and silver roofs and doors of gold.[2] This is only because of the insignificance of the *Dunya* in the Allah's eyes, on the one hand, and the insignificance of the disbelievers in His eyes on the other. The Messenger of Allah said, may the peace and blessings of Allah be upon him: "If

---

1. This is narrated in *Majmu' at az-Zawa'id* by Tabarani and the chain of narration is good.

2. See the following *ayats* and their explanation in this work: *"Were it not for the fact that people might become one nation, We would have assigned to those who reject the All-Merciful roofs of silver to their houses and stairways up which to climb and doors of silver to their houses and couches on which to recline, and ornaments of gold."* (*The Gold Ornaments*: 33-34)

the *Dunya* were worth even a gnat's wing, Allah would not have given the disbeliever even a drop of water to drink." This explains some of the features of the terrible scene depicted in *Surat al-A'raf* where Allah, may He be exalted, says: *"The Companions of the Fire will call out to the Companions of the Garden, 'Throw down some water to us or some of what Allah has given you as provision.' They will say, 'Allah has forbidden them to the rejectors of faith.'"* (7:49)

We find that the believer suffers in the *Dunya*. He is constricted as if someone were at his throat. Something is always disturbing his state. Why is Divine help delayed in coming? Where are the stores of Allah's mercy? Have they been closed off from him? Certainly not! It is simply a sign of Divine protection of the believer. Allah protects him from the world and its blight just as one of us might prevent the sick person from drinking out of love for him and for fear that the water would exacerbate his sickness.

In the picture painted in *Surat al-A'raf* ("The Ramparts"), we see the true worth of the world when the disbelievers seek and beg for water. I remember an honoured brother, may Allah have mercy on him, who was not only suffering from a certain illness but was suffering also in his family life. He asked me: "How is it that my illnesses are multiplying despite the fact that I fast, pray and pay *zakat* on my wealth?" I replied, "May Allah have mercy on you and me – do you wish to be protected from the calamities of the *Dunya* by your fasting, your prayer and your *zakat*? Or do you wish that your forbearance in the face of these calamities be stored up (for later reward) with your Lord?" We do not live in the Garden or in the abode of reward but in the abode of trial and testing. The reward and pleasure of Allah will be ours in the Next World.

'Abdullah ibn 'Amr ibn al-'As reported that the Messenger of Allah, may the peace and blessings of Allah be upon him, said: "He who submits, who is provided with sufficient provision, and whom Allah renders content with what He has given is successful."[1]

---

1. Reported by Imam Ahmad.

So the signs of success according to Allah are that one submit to Allah, may He be exalted; that one's provision be in proportion to his need – no more lest it lead to oppressive and arrogant behaviour, and no less lest it lead to deprivation; and that one is content with what he has and thereby free from any feelings of malice, envy, greed or any other of the illnesses of the heart.

> According to Abu Umama the Messenger of Allah, may the peace and blessings of Allah be upon him, reported, "The happiest of my friends (or in another narration "the happiest of people") with me is the believer who has little property or family, performs the full measure of prayers, worships his Lord in the best manner, and is hidden amongst people, no one pointing him out with his finger: and whose death comes early, whose inheritance is small and whose passing few mourn."[1]

These are the qualities possessed by those who have a high rank with Allah and His Messenger, may the peace and blessings of Allah be upon him. They have little property or family and so are not weighed down by any responsibility or by the chattels of this world. They perform their full measure of prayers, considering them to be of benefit and being concerned to profit as much as possible from them. They are hidden and unknown amongst people, having no rank or standing, so that there is no reason for others to point them out in public by saying that such and such a person enjoys such a such a position. Their death comes early so that they are still in the same very humble state when death overtakes them. Their inheritance will be small, meaning that they leave none of the fleeting things of this world or so little as to be of no significance.[2] There will be few mourners for them as they are hidden and unknown among people. It is all the same to others whether they are alive or dead.

---

1. Narrated by Ahmad.

2. Unless they leave a right-acting son who makes supplications for them or leave something they have paid for by *sadaqa* or leave behind an action which others profit by – these are the good actions which will carry on earning rewards for them after their death while they are in the grave.

In this *hadith* there is a clear sign that we should combat our natural tendency to be beguiled by the world. All the aspects of character indicated in this *hadith* will act as a cure for the arrogance which can enter the hearts of those of wealth and standing.

Al-'Abbas ibn Salim al-Lakhmi said that 'Umar ibn 'Abdal-'Aziz sent for Abu Salam al-Habashi who was brought to him by courier horse in order to ask him about the Basin (*al-Hawd*). When he was brought before him and questioned by 'Umar, he replied, "I heard Thawban say that he heard the Messenger of Allah say, may the peace and blessings of Allah be upon him: 'My Basin stretches from Adnin to Uman al-Balqa, its water is more intensely white than milk and sweeter than honey, its goblets are more numerous than the number of stars, and whoever takes a drink from it will never thirst again afterwards. The first people to come to drink from it will be the poor who made the *Hijra*.' Then 'Umar ibn al-Khattab asked, 'Who are they, Messenger of Allah? He replied, 'They are the ones with dishevelled and dusty hair and soiled clothes, those who have not married the affluent and fortunate and for whom the gates of abundance have not been opened.'" Then 'Umar ibn 'Abdu'l-'Aziz said, "I have married an affluent and fortunate woman and the gates have been opened for me – (so I shall not be among them) unless Allah has mercy on me.'"[1]

Who, then, are the first to come to drink at the Basin of the Messenger of Allah, may the peace and blessings of Allah be upon him? They are the poor, the poor who made *Hijra*. And how are they to be recognised?

They are dishevelled and their hair is covered in dust because of their travel through the land and their struggle in the Cause of Allah, unconcerned if their hair or their clothes get dirty. Their clothes are dirty but although they are dirty they are not impure, for purity is not mere outward cleanliness or brightness of the gar-

---

1. Narrated by Ahmad.

110

ments: rather, purity according to the Law means absence of any filth, both literal and metaphorical. They are people who have not married affluent women used to ease and comfort, not those who are only concerned with the outward aspects of beauty of such women and who therefore lose out in respect of the Next World. No doors have opened for them – that is, no doors of power and possession. They have great difficulty in gaining access to those in authority or in drawing the attention of those in authority to any problem they have. No one fears them as they have no strength or power and no place is secured for them.

Islam is the *deen* of cleanliness and purity and not the *deen* of extravagance and waste. It is more fitting for the believer to have soiled clothes than to be extravagant. A believer who is dishevelled and dusty is content with the minimum of clothes and does not mind that they are not bright and fresh as long as they are free of impurity. A man who has bright clothes and a pleasant appearance is of no worth if he eats pork or drinks wine.

A believer who has a dishevelled and dusty appearance disdains those who are dictated to by their whims and desire. The fact that he is not allowed to wear silk or may be unable to obtain grilled and roasted meat or delicacies does not worry him in any way. It is not a problem for him as he is not a person of such tastes. A dusty and dishevelled believer only has aspirations for his Lord and only seeks His pleasure, spending day and night seeking His good pleasure and acting out of obedience to Him alone. If the call to *Jihad* is given, he responds and hastens to it and if someone calls to him to expend his energy and wealth for something he gives without grudging. If the enemy want to crush or humiliate him he does not succumb to that in any way.

But a person who is dressed very finely but has a low and mean character, a person caught up in admiring his own appearance and who thinks too much about his clothes and other garments, such a person is concerned only to seek whatever accords with his sense of fashion and beauty. He is too busy for *Jihad* and any worship he might undertake is done only for show. He wastes his life and his actions disappear into thin air because of their insubstantial nature.

111

The dishevelled and dusty believer entrusts the reins of his mount in life to Allah alone whereas the man of extravagance and waste places his halter in the hands of anyone who will guarantee him his pleasures and will grant him immediate benefit and profit.

It is narrated from Abu Dharr that the Messenger of Allah, may the peace and blessings of Allah be upon him, asked, "Abu Dharr, which mountain is that?" He replied: "Uhud, O Messenger of Allah!" He said: "By the One in Whose Hand is my self, I would not like to have any gold at all which I was spending in the Cause of Allah if I were to leave a carat of it unspent." Abu Dharr said: "Did you mean a *qintar* of it, Messenger of Allah?" He replied, "No, a carat of it." He said this three times and then continued, "O Abu Dharr, I mean the smaller amount not the larger amount."

This is also reported from him in another narration: "I would not like to have the weight of Uhud in gold if on the day I died I still had a dinar or a half a dinar left, unless I were keeping it for a creditor."[1]

If Uhud were to be transmuted into gold it would surely be a great amount. Despite the amount, what would be the Prophet's way of spending this wealth? – spending it for the Cause of Allah until not even a carat remained. Abu Dharr, may Allah be pleased with him, was confused and asked if he meant a qintar but the Messenger of Allah, may the peace and blessings of Allah be upon him, emphasied that he had said a carat, emphasing this by repetition, and adding that he meant the smaller amount not the larger amount. By this he was indicating that the amount which entailed less of the *Dunya* is sufficient and whatever entails more is an excess. The second narration which includes the words "unless I were keeping it for a creditor" in effect grants permission for a part of the wealth to remain if there is a real need for it.

'Ali ibn Rabah said: "I heard 'Amr ibn al-'As, may Allah be pleased with him, say, 'Whenever you awake in

---

1. Narrated by Ahmad.

the morning or evening comes upon you are always desirous of what the Messenger of Allah, may the peace and blessings of Allah be upon him, did without. Whenever you awake in the morning or evening comes upon you, you are always desirous of the *Dunya* which the Messenger of Allah did without. By Allah, no night of his life came to him, may the peace and blessings of Allah be upon him, without him owing more than he had in his possession.' Then one of the Companions of the Messenger of Allah, may the peace and blessings of Allah be upon him said, 'He would borrow and contract loans.'"

It is not fitting that the believer should want for himself what the Messenger of Allah did not want for himself. Therefore if the Messenger of Allah did without in the *Dunya* and was only desirous of what was with Allah, then it is not fitting for any Muslim to be desirous of the *Dunya* or to be content with it or to feel secure in it, lest that cause him to forgo the Next World. If the Muslim does do this, it is dangerous for him. It is as if – and we seek refuge from Allah from it – he is belittling the judgement of those who have gone before him.[1]

The life of the Messenger of Allah, may the peace and blessings of Allah be upon him, is like a lantern which illuminates the way for people of intellect. We ask Allah, may He be exalted, to grant us the capacity to follow him as a model in the best manner.

Abu Umama relates that the Prophet, may the peace and blessings of Allah be upon him, said, "My Lord, may He be honoured, offered me the equivalent of the valley of Makka full of gold. I replied, 'No, O Lord! I would rather be full one day and be hungry the next. When I am hungry I will be humbled to You and remember You, and when I am full I will praise You and thank You.'"

---

1. It is reported that one of the signs of the Last Hour will be that the later generations will curse the first – with criticism and rejection – and we seek the refuge of Allah from that.

Anas ibn Malik said that he went into where the Prophet, may the peace and blessings of Allah be upon him, was lying on some thin palm matting with a skin stuffed with palm fibre beneath his head. Then 'Umar came in and the Messenger of Allah shifted his position. 'Umar could not see any clothing between his side and the matting and the matting had left its mark on the body of the Messenger of Allah, may the peace and blessings of Allah be upon him. 'Umar wept and then the Messenger of Allah asked, may the peace and blessings of Allah be upon him: "Why are you weeping, 'Umar?" He replied: "By Allah, it is nothing but the fact that I know that you are more honoured before Allah, may He be exalted, than Chosroes and Caesar who play in the world as they play – but you, Messenger of Allah, are in the position I see you in." Then the Messenger of Allah, may the peace and blessings of Allah be upon him, said, "Are you not content that they possess the *Dunya* and we have the Next World?" 'Umar said, "I certainly am!" He then said, "Then this is how it is."[1]

The Prophet wanted to teach his Community a profound lesson which any person of intellect and all those whom Allah wishes to guide will be able to profit from. Suffice it to point out that the Prophet, may the peace and blessings of Allah be upon him, was poor, that he suffered all the hardships of life and the restrictions imposed on him by those with authority and influence. All this happened to him during his life, may the peace and blessings of Allah be upon him, and should have been lesson enough for everyone.

The example he set in his life, however, is not always enough to affect some people. Some do not necessarily consider it as a model to be followed. His behaviour is not always enough to make them imitate him. But then there is the lesson which comes from Heaven, the most sublime of lessons. Allah offers His Prophet the choice of either being a king, independent and rich, and of still

---

1. This and the previous *hadith* are reported by Ahmad in his *Musnad*.

being the transmitter of the Message – or of being a poor person, a slave and a messenger.

Such an offer would excite anyone who was attached to this world but it does not deceive or beguile someone who bears a Divine Message. So the Messenger of Allah, may the peace and blessings of Allah be upon him, chose the path of slavehood. What is the reason for this? Because in independence and riches there is a severe test and trial. *"Surely man is inordinate in seeing himself as independent."* (96:6-7)

Poverty plays a positive role in the life of the believer and this positive element is manifest in the saying of the Prophet, may the peace and blessings of Allah be upon him: "O Lord, I prefer to be full one day and hungry the next." Is this a refusal of the blessings of Allah? Certainly not! It is simply that the Messenger realises that true blessings will come in the Next World. Is it that the Messenger of Allah fears the trials and testing of this *Dunya*? Again, certainly not! For he is the Messenger of Allah and Allah has guaranteed that He will protect him. It is he who said: "By the One in Whose Hand is my soul, I would not like to have any gold at all which I was spending for the Cause of Allah if I were to leave a carat of it unspent." This shows that he knows how to spend from the blessings of Allah. The Messenger explains the aim and purpose of his choice, may the peace and blessings of Allah be upon him by saying, "When I am hungry I will be humbled to You and remember You, and when I am full I will praise You and thank You."

His every state and circumstance is connected totally to his Lord, may He be exalted and praised. He brings his poverty and need before Allah just as his poverty brings him before Allah. The Messenger of Allah demonstrates for his Community the relation between need and proximity to Allah so that those who have a capacity for remembrance may remember.

Abu Nu'aym narrates in *al-Hilya* from 'Urwa that 'Umar ibn al-Khattab came into where Abu 'Ubayda ibn al-Jarrah was, may Allah be pleased with both of them. Abu 'Ubayda was lying down on the coarse shaggy saddle cloth of his mount using his saddle bag as a pillow. 'Umar said, "Do you not want to use what your companions use (when resting)?" He replied: "Amir of the Believers, this is enough for my midday rest." (Ma'mar in his narration of the *hadith* said): "When 'Umar went to Sham (Syria) he met the people as well as the great and influential persons of the land and he asked, "Where is my brother?" They replied, "Who do you mean?" He said: "Abu 'Ubayda." They said, "He is coming to you now." When he arrived, 'Umar dismounted and embraced him and went into his house. He saw nothing in his house but his sword, his shield and his mount – and then he described (what he saw) in a similar way to that (in the other *hadith*).[1]

Abu 'Ubayda, may Allah be pleased with him, followed the Prophet's lesson and had understood the aim and purpose of the life of the *Dunya*: that this world was the abode of pleasure, that it was the bridge to the Next World and that the provision of the traveller is enough for the believer. Abu 'Ubayda, may Allah be pleased with him, had established himself in Sham which is a land of great abundance and wealth. It would have been possible for him to acquire wealth but he explains his purpose in having so few belongings when he says, "This is enough for my midday rest." We realise that he is only concerned with the present, like a traveller on the road. We see that his sword, his shield and his mount will be all he needs after his midday rest.

> *"O you who believe, do not let your wealth and your children distract you from the remembrance of Allah: whoever does so will be losers."* (63:9)

The believer should not allow himself to be chained to this life, nor should he cut himself off from obtaining the means to his freedom and salvation. Wealth and children are the adornment of the life of this world. It is precisely this adornment which enslaves

---

1. The author of *Sifa al-Safwa* says that this is reported by Imam Ahmad while according to *al-Isaba* it is narrated from Ibn Mubarak in the section on Detachment – and this has been taken from the *Life of the Companions* by Kandhilawi.

man and takes him captive through his love for them. He becomes in effect a prisoner of his desires and passions. Sincerity is only achieved by the believer by means of remembrance of Allah, may He be exalted.

Is it permitted for love of wealth and children to overcome man and for him to become preoccupied with them to the detriment of his remembrance of Allah? Surely not. If that happens, he will find himself in a state of clear loss. It is not rational for a believer to prefer the pleasures of this world to the remembrance of Allah, may He be exalted. A believer should be concerned for his own freedom and this freedom will not be achieved unless he is concerned to maintain his faith. It is his faith in Allah which is the measure of the value of his life in the *Dunya*; it is his faith in Allah which is the source of his freedom; it is his faith in Allah which will be his salvation from torment on the Day of Resurrrection.

> Abu Sa'id al-Khudri said that the Messenger of Allah said, may the peace and blessings of Allah be upon him: "Whoever has little wealth and a large family and performs the prayers well and does not slander Muslims will be with me on the Day of Resurrection."[1]

This *hadith* shows the Muslim how to be patient in the face of the difficulties of this world. The first characteristic is to have little wealth because of the trial and testing incurred by having much and because of the tendency of the human soul to attach itself to this wealth. The second is to have a large family because of all this entails in the way of struggling and striving to see to their needs. Thirdly, one is able to overcome the difficulties of the *Dunya* by the correct performance of the prayer if, despite his poverty and his family, he offers the prayers at their proper time and does not hasten to get them over with like a hen pecking at the ground. The fourth characteristic is to keep one's tongue free from backbiting. One must not see the faults of other people as one should be preoccupied with his own faults. One must not criticise others as he should be concerned with his own state with Allah – by remember-

---

1. This is cited in *Majmu'at az-Zawa'id*.

ing Him and praising Him. On the Last Day such a man will be with the Messenger of Allah, may the peace and blessings of Allah be upon him, in the highest Garden of Paradise.

Those desirous of this world and the Next World

> *"Everything in the heavens and everything in the earth belongs to Allah. Allah is enough as a guardian. If He willed He could remove you altogether, O mankind, and produce others instead. Allah is more than capable of doing that. If anyone desires the reward of this world, the reward of this world and the Next World are with Allah. Allah is All-Hearing, All-Seeing."* (4:131-3)

Allah is watching to see what each person earns for himself. He is the One Who witnesses all things and He is capable of removing you and replacing you with others if you disobey, as He says: *"If you turn away He will replace you with a people other than you and they will not be like you."* (47:40) There is nothing more insignificant in the sight of Allah than His slaves when they are negligent in carrying out His orders. He says, may He be exalted: *'Allah is more than capable of doing that...'* in other words, He is not incapable of changing a whole people. He also says: *'If anyone desires the reward of this world, the reward of this world and the Next World is with Allah.'* People who have inclination and yearning only for this world should know that Allah possesses the reward for this world and the Next World. Provided your heart is attached to the Next World, if you ask Him for something He will grant it you and will enrich you and make you content.

> *"There are some people who say, 'Our Lord, give us good in this world.' They will have no share in the Next World. And there are others who say, 'Our Lord, give us good in this world, and good in the Next World, and guard us from the punishment of the Fire.' They shall have a good share from what they have earned. Allah is swift at reckoning."* (2:199-200)

"The reward of this world and the Next World is with Allah."
This is clear proof that all good in both worlds is to be obtained
from His hand alone. So do not restrict yourself to striving after
the *Dunya* but rather let your aspirations and endeavour be
towards obtaining the highest of goals in this world and the Next;
for surely the source of all this is the One in Whose Hand is both
harm and benefit. It is He, Allah, Who has apportioned happiness
and unhappiness to people in this world and the Next. It is He
Who judges with justice between those who are entitled to one
particular thing and others who are entitled to something else.

> Zayd ibn Thabit says, relating a *hadith* of the Prophet,
> may the peace and blessings of Allah be upon him:
> "Whoever makes this world his intention, Allah will put
> his poverty between his eyes and will disperse his posses-
> sions, and only what has been written for him will come to
> him. Whoever makes his intention the Next World, He
> will make him rich and independent in his heart, his pos-
> sessions will be enough for him and this world will come
> to him even though he is averse to it."[1]

This *hadith* demonstrates the diversity of man's direction and
purpose. People who are attached to the *Dunya* are constantly on
the lookout for poverty, and because of this poverty manifests in
their every circumstance and state. They are always in need and
never content with anything, as they want everything but can never
obtain more than a fraction of what they want. If you seek this
world poverty will constantly loom before you as an enemy. But if
you are attached to the Next World you will become independent
of this world and see it at its true worth.

Your material possessions and the pleasures of this world will
not amount to anything significant in your eyes since you will see
them merely as means of crossing over to the Next World and will
not desire any more of them than is necessary to gain your salvation in the Next World. When that is the case you will find that this

---

1. According to al-Bayhaqi part of this *hadith* is related by Ibn Majah. At-
Tabarani has also related it in *al-Awsat* and his transmitters are trustworthy.

world comes to you, despite your turning from it, so that you will always obtain sufficient provision from it.

Abu'd-Darda' reported that the Messenger of Allah, may the peace and blessings of Allah be upon him, said, "Be free of the cares of this world as much as you can, for surely Allah will disperse the possessions and place poverty before the eyes of the person whose greatest concern is this world. As for the person whose greatest concern is the Next World, Allah will arrange matters in his favour and will give him wealth and riches in his heart. No one turns to Allah with his heart without Allah causing the hearts of the believers to incline towards him with love and mercy and Allah being very swift to bring him all that is good."[1]

This *hadith* emphasises and explains the meanings contained in the previous *hadiths*. Here, as in the other *hadiths*, is a warning against attaching yourself to this ephemeral world lest a connection to your possessions cause you to be dispersed in your intention and lest the horrible spectre of poverty materialise before you and put your life constantly under threat. It also contains a stimulus towards the Next World. Attachment to the Next World, we learn, guarantees a person serenity and tranquillity in this world just as it guarantees blessing and fortune in the Gardens beneath which rivers flow.

The *hadith* next goes on to explain the excellence of turning to Allah, may He be exalted, with the heart in sincerity and certainty. In response Allah will join the hearts of the believers to other persons of sincerity and surround them with love and mercy. Not only that, but Allah will guarantee them all the best of this world and the Next in the shortest possible time.

Anas reported that the Messenger of Allah said, may the peace and blessings of Allah be upon him: "Whoever makes this world the object of his concern and love, the thing for which he is keenly on the watch, and the end

1. This is reported in *Majmu'at az-Zawa'id* and at-Tabarani narrates it in *al-Kabir* and *al-Awsat*.

towards which his aim and purpose directs him, Allah will place poverty before his eyes and will cause his possessions to be dispersed. Nothing of these possessions will come to him except that which has been written for him. Whoever makes the Next World his concern and love, that for which he is keenly on the watch and the thing towards which his aim and purpose directs him, Allah, may He be exalted, will place riches and wealth in his heart and will gather together his possessions; and this world will come to him in a state of submission."[1]

This *hadith* is very similar to those already quoted and re-emphasises them. Surely actions are judged by intentions so reflect what will be the consequence if your intention is directed towards the *Dunya* and attached to it. Poverty will be always be close to you because those who seek after the world always see poverty before them.[2] Your possessions will be dispersed and split up. You will become unsure about what you should do and your aim and purpose in life will become confused. In any case, no matter how grandiose your plans or how vigorous your efforts you can only obtain what has been written and decreed for you.

But if you are someone who seeks after the Next World your heart will become enriched and independent. Your aim and purpose will not become fragmented and dispersed in your search for the *Dunya* since its sole intent is the Next World. You will then find that it is this world which comes to you in a state of humility and submission, and you will be its master and not its slave.

Anas reports that the Messenger of Allah declared, may the peace and blessings of Allah be upon him: "Whoever makes his intention the next world, Allah, may He be praised and blessed, will give riches and independence to

---

1. According to al-Haythami at-Tabarani narrates this in *al-Awsat* with two chains of narrations, in one of which is Dawud ibn al-Mihbar and in the other Ayyub ibn Hawt; both of them are very weak transmitters.

2. Reflect upon the meaning of this in relation to people who complain of the increase in the cost of living and their incapacity to get the things they want: their expenditure increases and money itself decreases in worth; and complaining increases; and so it is as if such people were in a constant state of poverty.

his heart, He will arrange his every concern and will remove poverty from his eyes; this world will come to him despite his aversion to it and he will not awake of a morning without being rich and independent and evening will not arrive for him but that he will be rich and independent. Whoever makes this world his intention, Allah will place poverty before his eyes and he will always awake as a poor person and evening will not arrive for him without him being a poor person."[1]

This is yet another *hadith* from a different source exactly confirming those which have immediately preceded it.

Abu Musa al-Ash'ari relates that the Messenger of Allah, may the peace and blessings of Allah be upon him, said: "Whoever loves his *Dunya* harms his *Akhira* and whoever loves his *Akhira* harms his *Dunya* and prefers what lasts to what is ephemeral."[2]

This *hadith* urges the believer to be in a constant state of preparedness. It exhorts him to give precedence to his Next World and to prefer what endures to what vanishes. It is one of the strangest things that a person can spend hundreds of thousands of pounds on a grand building or factory and bequeath it to those who will inherit from him but then be mean and niggardly in paying the *zakat* which is the right of Allah, may He be exalted. It is even stranger when you consider that those who do pay *zakat* are guaranteed the fullest of recompense from Allah, may He be exalted, on the Day of Resurrection.

On one occasion 'A'isha, may Allah be pleased with her, gave away all of her portion from the *Bayt al-Mal* treasury, forgetting to leave anything over to buy some food with and she was fasting at the time. When her slave-girl chided her about this she said, "If you had reminded me about that I would have done it."

1. Al-Haythami says that this is narrated by al-Bazzaz, although in the chain of narration is Isma'il ibn Muslim al-Makki who is weak; but it may be that this narration purifies and ameliorates the previous one. Allah knows best.
2. Narrated by Ahmad and al-Bazzar and at-Tabarani, whose transmitters are trustworthy as al-Bayhaqi says.

The family of the Prophet, may the peace and blessings of Allah be upon him, sacrificed a sheep, gave away some of its meat as *sadaqa* but kept the shoulder for the Prophet may the peace and blessings of Allah be upon him, who liked this (part of the sheep). When the Messenger of Allah arrived, may the peace and blessings of Allah be upon him, they informed him that only the shoulder of the sheep remained and he said, may the peace and blessings of Allah be upon him, "It is true that none of the sheep remains except for the shoulder but in reality it is the *sadaqa* which remains."

Many of the Companions and the *Salihun*, may Allah be pleased with them, gave away their wealth as *sadaqa* and they gave of themselves for the Cause of Allah. 'Uthman, may Allah be pleased with him, spent of his wealth to equip the so-called Army of Difficulty (as the expeditionary force to Tabuk is called because it was sent in the hottest season) so much so that the Mes-senger, may the peace and blessings of Allah be upon him, said: "Nothing that 'Uthman does after this will be of any harm to him."

Another time 'Uthman bought a well from a Jew and established it for the benefit of the Muslims. It belonged originally to this Jew charged extortionate prices for its water. The Prophet, may the peace and blessings of Allah be upon him, wanted to buy it and so then 'Uthman wanted to buy it. The Jew refused to sell it outright but he was prepared to sell half of it, which 'Uthman bought. 'Uthman then allowed the Muslims to take as much as they wished from it for free on the days allotted to him, which saved them from having to buy it from the Jew. He then realised that 'Uthman had ruined (the business of) the well for him and so he sold it all to him. Then 'Uthman made it over to the Muslims. The name of the well was the Ruma Well.

The Messenger of Allah spoke the truth when he said: "Whoever loves his Next World does harm to his *Dunya*."

What should we think when we see so many people nowadays who hold wealth in such high esteem but who then refuse to pay the *zakat*? The intellects of such people have been dulled by extravagance and luxury and they forget the darkness and constriction of the grave; they forget the severity of the Reckoning. The

Qur'an describes these people who by their actions show that they think this world will last forever. *"Do you build a tower on every headland, to amuse yourselves, and construct great fortresses, hoping to live for ever?"* (26:128-9)

> It is narrated from Shurayh ibn 'Ubayda al-Hadrami that Abu Malik al-Ash'ari said on his death-bed, "O you among the Ash'aris who can hear and are obedient, let those of you who are present tell those who are absent that I heard the Messenger of Allah, may the peace and blessings of Allah be upon him, say, "The sweetness of this world is bitterness in the Next World and the bitterness of this world is sweetness in the Next World."[1]

So whoever wishes the Next World to be good and pleasant for him should put up with the burden and sufferings of this world and make his actions in it for the sake of Allah's pleasure. He should spend in the Cause of Allah; he should rise in the night to come close to Allah by means of prayer; he should perform *Jihad* in the Way of Allah; he should be truthful whenever he bears witness. All these things, however difficult they sometimes are to carry out, contain good, and the believer will harvest the fruit of such actions in the Next World.

> *"Allah is gentle with His slaves. He provides for anyone He wills, and He is the Strong, the Mighty. Whoever desires the harvest of the Next World, We will increase him in his harvest. Whoever desires the harvest of this world, We will give him something of it, but in the Next World there will be no share for him."* (42:17-18)

This is a warning: love of this world, attachment to it and reliance on it alone means inevitable doom and destruction. As for those who want the Next World and its harvest, Allah will increase them in their harvest but those who restrict themselves to this world and limit their endeavour and striving to it alone will receive only what has already been decreed for them and, on top of this,

---

1. Al-Haythami says that this is narrated by Ahmad and at-Tabarani and their transmitters are trustworthy.

they will be deprived of the Next World. So reflect on the dangerous nature of certain desires and tendencies of the heart; and remember that at this point we are merely discussing desires and tendencies and have not begun to discuss the sphere of actions. If someone only desires the *Dunya* exclusively, that desire alone will be the cause of his losing both this world and the Next.

According to Ibn Kathir[1] "the harvest of the Next World" refers to what is obtained as a result of actions undertaken for the Next World. The words: "We will increase him in his harvest" means that Allah will help him to achieve what he intends and He will reward him at least ten times in return for every good action – up to as much as seven hundred times or as Allah wishes. The words "Whoever desires the harvest of this world, We will give him something of it, but in the Next World there will be no share for him" means that whoever strives to obtain something in this world and has no concern at all for the Next World will be forbidden the Next World. As for the *Dunya,* he will be given it if Allah wills but if He does not wish him to be given of it he will get neither of the two; so the one who strives with this intent will lose out in both worlds. The Prophet, may the peace and blessings of Allah be upon him, said: "Give good news to this *Umma* of sublimity and elevation, victory and firm establishment on the earth. But whoever does an action which is ostensibly for the Next World which is actually for the sake of this world will have no portion in the Next World."

> *"When you have completed your rites, remember Allah*
> *as you used to remember your forefathers, or even more.*
> *There are some people who say, "Our Lord, give us good*
> *in this world." They will have no share in the Next World.*
> *And there are others who say, "Our Lord, give us good in*
> *this world, and good in the Next World, and guard us from*
> *the punishment of the Fire." They will have a good share*
> *from what they have earned. Allah is swift at reckoning."*
> (2:199-200)

---

1. In his commentary, vol. 4, p. 119.

Life is gift from Allah, may He be exalted – one of the many that He has granted mankind. *"And if you count the blessings of Allah you cannot number them."* (16:18) There are those who are beguiled by ephemeral blessings and are heedless of the blessings which are eternal. Such people have no portion of the Next World. There is another group however, who are not distracted by the affairs of this world to the detriment of the Next World and it is they who call on their Lord saying: "O our Lord, give us good in this world and good in the Next World, and protect us from the punishment of the Fire."

The good of this world means beneficial provision, good health and any other good associated with these two things. The good of the next world is the Garden, after the person concerned has gained safety from the Great Terror (of the Reckoning). The search for what is good in the Next World is closely connected to the search for salvation from the Fire, for it is necessary to have an attachment to what is blessed and a fear of the painful torment. Allah says, may He be exalted: *"Whoever is removed from the Fire and is brought into the Garden has gained victory."* Thus the concern of the believer is to strive in the life of the *Dunya* while not becoming heedless of the states of the Next World. The hand of the believer is on this world while his heart is in the Next World.

Allah, may He be exalted, has exhorted people to call on Him and to remember Him a great deal. But He is aware what the response of many will be. He belittles those who only call on Him for matters of this world and are heedless of the Next World, saying: "There are some people who say, 'Our Lord, give us good in this world.' They will have no share in the Next World."

Sa'id ibn Jubayr narrates from Ibn 'Abbas that some of the Bedouin Arabs would come to Makka and say, "O Allah, make this year a year of rains, a year of fertile land, a year good for childbirth" without mentioning anything about matters of the Next World. Then Allah revealed this *ayat*. Others who were believers would come saying, "O our Lord give us good in the *Dunya* and good in the Next World and protect us from the punishment of the

Fire." Then Allah, may He be exalted, revealed: "They will have a good share from what they have earned".

This supplication encompasses all the good in the world and averts all the evil. The good mentioned in the supplication includes all that may be desired in this world: that is, good health, a welcoming home, a good wife, ample provision, beneficial knowledge, a decent occupation, a modest mount and all those things which are laudable and commended and are mentioned in the works of the commentators. There is no incompatibility or inconsistency between any of these things for they are all encompassed by the Arabic term *hasana*, meaning what is good.

As for the *hasana* of the Next World, the highest of these is entry into the Garden and all that pertains to it: that is, safety and security from the Great Terror in the places where the Reckoning takes place, the making easy of this Reckoning, and all other aspects of a fortunate end in the Next World. Al-Qasim Abu 'Ubayd Abu 'Abd ar-Rahman said, "Whoever is given a grateful heart, a tongue active in remembrance and a body capable of patience and forbearance has been given the good of this world and the good of the Next World and will be protected from the torment of the Fire."[1]

> Abu Hurayra narrates that the Messenger of Allah said, may the peace and blessings of Allah be upon him: "O Allah make the provision of my household sufficient for one day (at a time)." And in a second narration, "O Allah, make the provision for the family of Muhammad sufficient for one day."

> Anas relates that the Messenger of Allah said, peace and blessings be upon him: "There will be no one on the Day of Resurrection, be they rich or poor, who would not have preferred to have been given (only) a day's provision."

> Fadala ibn 'Ubayd narrates that when the Messenger of Allah, may the peace and blessings of Allah be upon him, used to lead the people in prayer some men would fall from their standing position in the prayer because of their

1. Ibn Kathir, *Tafsir*, vol. 1, pp. 252-3.

extreme state of penury. They were from among those known as the Companions of the Bench (*Ahl as-Suffa*) and some Bedouin Arabs even went so far as to say they were mad. When the Messenger of Allah, may the peace and blessings of Allah be upon him, finished the prayer, he would go to them saying, "If you only knew what there is with Allah for you, you would wish your need and poverty to increase." Fadala said, "And I was with the Messenger of Allah, may the peace and blessings of Allah be upon him, that day."

Abu Sa'id al-Khudri narrates that the Prophet said, may the peace and blessings of Allah be upon him, that Musa, on whom be peace and blessings, said: "O Lord, Your believing slave is compelled to live in straitened circumstances in this world." Then the gate of Paradise was opened for him (by Allah) and he looked inside. Allah then said, "O Musa, this is what I have prepared for him." Musa replied, "O Lord, by Your power and Your majesty, even if both his hands and legs were cut off and he were dragged along from the day he was created until the Day of Resurrection and that were the course of his life, he still would not consider it the least calamity or wretchedness." Musa continued, "O Lord, this world extends itself liberally for Your disbelieving slave." Then the gate of the Fire was opened for him (by Allah), and He said, "O Musa, this is what I have prepared for him." Then Musa said, "O Lord, by Your power and Your majesty, even if he were to possess the whole of this world from the day. You created him until the Day of Resurrection and that were the course of his life, he would not see any goodness in it."[1]

These *hadiths* touch upon three matters. The first is the question of a model to be imitated. That model appears in the supplication of the Best of Creation, Muhammad, may the peace and blessings of Allah be upon him. "O Allah, make the provision of my household sufficient for one day (at a time)." Here he, may the

1. Narrated by Imam Ahmad and the author of *al-Fath ar-Rabbani*.

peace and blessings of Allah be upon him, is setting up an example to be followed by his Community. If the *Dunya* were worth anything in the balance and in the estimation of Allah then the Messenger, may the peace and blessings of Allah be upon him, would have been the first among people to desire it and to hold on to it and to call upon Allah to increase him in it; but in fact he merely asks Allah to make the provision for his household enough for a single day's provision.

The second matter is the question of what really constitutes a blessing. This is made clear from the good news given by the Messenger of Allah to those poor persons who, out of weakness and poverty, used to fall where they were stood in the prayer. So the relationship between the blessings of this world and those of the Next is one of opposites, in the sense that the more luxury and blessings people have in the *Dunya* the more their portion in the *Akhira* is liable to be diminished; and the less luxury or comfort people have in this world the more their portion in the Next Life is likely to be.

The truth of the situation is depicted for us by the Prophet, may the peace and blessings of Allah be upon him, when he makes it clear that on the Day of Resurrection everyone – both rich and poor – will have only one desire. When they see the terror of the Reckoning which will take account of their every smallest of possession in this lower world, they will all wish that their provision had been apportioned in such a way that each day they had only had enough for that day.

In the *hadith* about Musa, on whom be peace, a clear truth is made manifest. He wished to know why a believer should be compelled to live in straitened circumstances in the *Dunya* and why this world extended liberally for a disbeliever. He was answered by the gate of the Garden being opened to allow him to see the blessings the believer can expect in the Next World with the result that all his misfortune diminishes to the point of disappearance. This caused Musa to say that even if the believer had a life of the most agonising torture he would not consider it the least hardship when he finds the blessings which were in store for him. And indeed all of us have had a taste of this: when a time of great pain or misery is followed by relief and ease it is sometimes almost as if the difficult time had never happened.

In reply to his second question one of the gates of the Fire is opened to allow Musa, on whom be peace, to see what the disbeliever can expect – the disbeliever for whom the *Dunya* has extended itself so liberally and for whom the doors of luxury and extravagance have been opened. When he sees what is awaiting the unbeliever Musa exclaims, "O Lord, by Your power and Your majesty, even if he were to possess the whole world from the day You created him until the Day of Resurrection and that was the course of his life he would not see any goodness in it."

> Mahmud ibn Labid narrates that the Prophet observed, may the peace and blessings of Allah be upon him: "Two things are disliked by the son of Adam: death, although death is better than trial and discord; and lack of wealth, although lack of wealth means there is less for him to be called to account for."[1]

Islam calls upon the believer to use his intellect to obtain the good of this world and the Next. The Qur'an warns man that too much kindly benevolence is not always a good thing but that neither is it always a bad thing, for it may well be that there is good in what we dislike and bad in what we like. Allah, may He be exalted, says: *"It may be that you hate a thing when it is good for you and it may be that you love a thing when it is bad for you."* (2:214)

The above-mentioned *hadith* explains this by saying that the son of Adam dislikes death even though death is better for him than exposing himself to trials and tribulations. Such trials may well be the cause of his losing much of the good he has gained in his life or of his being exposed to evil and even disbelief on occasions. Allah says, may He be exalted: *"Trials and tribulations (fitna) are worse than killing."* The believer dislikes having little wealth although it is an advantage for him since it means he will have less to account for. Moreover, lack of wealth often increases the soundness of his heart and his certainty. We have read in the

---

1. In *Majmu'at az-Zawa'id* it is stated that Ahmad narrates this with two narrations, and the narraters of one of them are sound.

guidance of the Prophet that the poor will enter the Garden half a day before the rich. That means five hundred years before them since Allah, may He be exalted, says: *"A day with your Lord is the same as a thousand years in the way you count."* (22:47)

Abu Usama narrates that he went to a place called Rabadha where Abu Dharr was and found him with an ugly black woman who had no trace on her of saffron coloured clothes or the perfume thereof. Abu Dharr said, "Do you see what this little black lady is commanding me to do? She is commanding me to come to Iraq. But if I were to go to Iraq they would make me have a predilection for their *Dunya*. But my friend, may the peace and blessings of Allah be upon him, assured me that the Bridge over Hellfire was a path which is slippery and treacherous and that if we came upon it with only a moderate or light burden we would be more likely to get across safely than if we were carrying heavy loads."[1]

Abu'd-Darda' narrates that the Messenger of Allah, may the peace and blessings of Allah be upon him, said: "Before you there is a difficult climb and only the lightly-burdened will reach the top."[2]

It is narrated from Anas that the Messenger of Allah, came out to them one day holding the hand of Abu Dharr and said: "I have given warning that there is a difficult ascent before us and only those who travel light will be able to climb it." Then a man said, "O Messenger of Allah, am I one of those travelling light or one of those weighed down with burdens?" He replied, "Do you have food enough for today?" He said, "Yes." "And food enough for tomorrow?" He replied, "Yes." "And food enough for the day after tomorrow?" He said, "No." He said, "If you had had food enough for three days then you would have been among the heavily burdened."[3]

---

1. This is narrated by Ahmad and his transmitters are sound.
2. This is narrated by al-Bazzar and his narraters are trustworthy.
3. At-Tabarani relates this in *al-Awsat* with a chain of narration that includes

131

From these *hadiths* the extent to which the Messenger of Allah, may the peace and blessings of Allah be upon him, would go to give directions and advice to his *Umma* so as to prevent them from going astray is very clear. This is because the *Dunya* is sweet whereas the Next World is in the Unseen and the road to it is full of pitfalls and very rough. Above Hellfire there is a dangerous bridge and a difficult ascent and this path is a slippery one from which many fall. People will be questioned about everything they obtained in the *Dunya*. How will they get to the end of this slippery path if they are encumbered[1] with heavy burdens? How will they be able to save themselves if their every step is weighed down with baggage?

Reflect on how Abu Dharr understood the Messenger of Allah, may the peace and blessings of Allah be upon him. He refused to go to Iraq for fear that doing so would give him a liking for the *Dunya* and thus make him one of those weighed down with encumbrances.

> Abu Umama reported, "The Messenger of Allah said, may the peace and blessings of Allah be upon him: 'O people, come to your Lord. Whatever is small in quantity and sufficient (for one's needs) is better than what is great in quantity and becomes a distraction. O people, these two possibilities represent two paths: the path of good and the path of evil. So what could possibly make the path of evil more beloved to you than the path of good?'"

This *hadith* explains the way to reach Allah, may He be exalted, the way to gain proximity to Him. This path to Allah and the means of staying on it will never be achieved by anyone who harbours a love of this world or in a state of preoccupation or distraction with it, or who is attached to its pleasures. It is for this reason that the Prophet says that what is small in quantity and is sufficient for one's needs is better than what is great in quantity and becomes a distraction. The path of good is clear and close by, and so the

Junada ibn Marwan, of whom Abu Hatim says that he is not strong although the rest of his men are trustworthy.

1. According to al-Haythami at-Tabarani narrates this from a *hadith* of Fadl from Abu Umama, and Fadl is considered weak.

Prophet asks why people should like the path of evil more than the path of good. The question is posed in astonishment that anyone could prefer it. It is also a rejection of such behaviour and a warning against it. It is as if the Prophet, may the peace and blessings of Allah be upon him, is warning and cautioning the believers lest they become attached to the *Dunya* and all the evil that it entails.

Mu'adh ibn Jabal narrates that when the Messenger of Allah, may the peace and blessings of Allah be upon him, sent him to the Yemen, he said, "Be careful not to procure yourself a life of ease, for surely the true slaves of Allah are not those who live easeful lives."

Abu 'Usayb said that one night the Messenger of Allah went out and "He passed me, called me to him and I came out. Then he passed Abu Bakr and called him and he went out to him. Then he passed 'Umar and called him and he went out to him. Then he went on until he entered a garden belonging to one of the Ansar and said to him, "Feed us some fresh dates." So the latter came with a cluster of them and placed them before him, and the Messenger of Allah, may the peace and blessings of Allah be upon him, and his Companions ate them. Then he called for cold water and then drank saying, "You will be questioned about this on the Day of Resurrection." Then 'Umar took the cluster of dates and struck them on the ground so that the fresh dates spread out in front of the Messenger of Allah, may the peace and blessings of Allah be upon him. He asked, "Messenger of Allah, will we too be questioned about this on the Day of Resurrection?" He replied, "Yes, (you will be asked about everything) except for three things: a patched garment with which a man covers his private parts, a slice of bread with which he quells his hunger and a space (of his home) which heat and cold penetrate."[1]

Mu'adh ibn Jabal listened to the advice of the Messenger of Allah, may the peace and blessings of Allah be upon him, warning

---

1. This is narrated by Ahmad in his *Musnad*.

him not to adopt a life of extravagance and luxury, for such a life is destructive and tears nations apart and makes people preoccupied with the tawdry insignificant aspects of this world. It makes them forget matters of import, forget the real purpose and aim of life. Blessings – that is, any of the good and beneficial things of life – will all be asked about on the Day of Resurrection: *"Then you will certainly be asked about blessings on that Day."* (102:8)

The danger of luxury and extravagance

At-Tirmidhi narrated – and he considered the narration to be good – and Abu Ya'la and Ibn Rahawayh also narrated from 'Ali, may Allah be pleased with him: "I went out one cold morning from my house and I was hungry, craving (for something to eat) and the cold had much weakened me, so I took a cut skin which we had with us and wrapped it round me like a jacket and then drew it up to my neck and secured it to my chest in order to warm me. By Allah, there was nothing to eat in my house and if there had been anything in the house of the Prophet, may the peace and blessings of Allah be upon him, he would have sent me some. I went out to one of the outlying parts of Madina and I saw a Jew in his garden through a hole in his wall. He said, 'O Arab, what about a date for every bucket (of water)?' I replied, 'Yes,' so he opened the (gate in the) wall for me to come in and I did so. Then I drew up the bucket and (for each bucket) he would give me a date until I had filled my palm. I then said, 'I have had enough from you,' and then I ate them and drank some water.

Then I came to the Prophet, may the peace and blessings of Allah be upon him, and sat down beside him in the mosque. He was amongst a group of companions and Mus'ab ibn 'Umayr, may Allah be pleased with him, also came up to this (group), wearing a patched cloak. When the Messenger of Allah, may the peace and blessings of Allah be upon him, caught sight of Mus'ab, he mentioned

134

what a blessing was to be found in it and when he saw his condition, his eyes filled with tears and he wept saying, 'How would you like to be able to go out in the morning wearing one garment and go out in the evening in another and for your houses to be just as protected as the Ka'ba?' We replied, 'That day we would be in a good state. Our provision would be sufficient and we would be able to devote ourselves entirely to worship.' He said: 'Today your state is better than that day.'"[1]

Here we have the story of two people: 'Ali ibn Abi Talib and Mus'ab ibn 'Umayr, may Allah be pleased with them. 'Ali was suffering from the cold and from hunger and was happy to accept the wage of a date in return for every bucket filled, until, that is, his hand was full, at which point he decided he had obtained sufficient and so he ate them and drank. Then he joined the Messenger of Allah, may the peace and blessings of Allah be upon him. Mus'ab ibn 'Umayr, may Allah be pleased with him, also joined the gathering looking so poor that the Messenger of Allah, may the peace and blessings of Allah be upon him, wept on mentioning the state he was in. The Messenger, may the peace and blessings of Allah be upon him, then warned those present that extravagance and luxury are of no value and of no help to worship, as they do not allow people to devote themselves to worship but instead pre-occupy the heart with love of this world and reliance on it.

He explained to them that it was better that their state should be one of poverty. Although it might appear that a life of ease would give one more free time he makes it clear that such free time lends itself to a waste of one's energies and usually leads one away from matters of faith and belief. A lavish lifestyle encourages the person concerned to feel at home in the life of this world, to find contentment with it and to covet it, all of which weakens a person's certainty.

So we see how the Messenger of Allah, may the peace and blessing of Allah be upon him, wept at the state of Mus'ab ibn

---

1. Al-Kandhilawi narrates it from *al-Kanz*, vol. 3, p. 321. It is also narrated from al-Bayhaqi who states that it is related from Abu Ya'la, and in the chain of narration there is an unnamed person while all the other men are trustworthy.

'Umayr who had been renowned in Makka for the beauty of his appearance, the sweetness of his perfume and the splendour of his person . His clothes were made of silk and his perfumes were of the costliest kind but he became a Muslim and followed the path of belief and trust. Faith suffused his heart and he discovered a sweetness in it which in turn suffused his spirit. He experienced a pleasure in comparison with which all other pleasures he had known receded into insignificance. The sweetness of faith made the beauty of outward appearance unimportant to him.

Allah revealed the words: *"Among the believers are men who have been true to the contract they made with Allah. Some have fulfilled their pact by death and some are still waiting to do so and have not changed in any way,"* (33:23) in order to confirm the high station of Mus'ab ibn 'Umayr and those of a similar state and condition. May Allah be pleased with them all.

Ahmad and al-Bazzar relate from Abu Dharr, may Allah be pleased with him, that he said: "The Prophet, may the peace and blessings of Allah be upon him, was addressing people when a bedouin Arab of rough appearance got up and said, 'O Messenger of Allah, a year of dearth has afflicted us.' The Prophet, may the peace and blessings of Allah be upon him, replied, 'Something other than that makes me more afraid for you – when the *Dunya* descends upon people in liberal quantities and they are unable to free themselves of their attachment to gold.'"[1]

The two Shaykhs (Muslim and al-Bukhari) narrate that Abu Sa'id al-Khudri, may Allah be pleased with him, said in a *hadith*, "The Messenger of Allah, may the peace and blessings of Allah be upon him, sat on the minbar and when we were sitting round him he said, 'What I fear for you is that Allah will open up for you the flower and beauty of the *Dunya*.'"

Abu Ya'la and al-Bazzar narrate from Sa'd ibn Abi Waqqas, may Allah be pleased with him, that the Messenger of Allah, may the peace and blessings of Allah be

---

1. *At-Targhib* states that the narrators of Ahmad are sound narrators.

upon him, said, "Truly I am more afraid for you of the trial of joys and pleasures than of the trial of difficulties and hardship. You have been put to the test by difficulties and hardship and you endured them but surely the *Dunya* is sweet and green."

Reflect, then, on what the Messenger, may the peace and blessings of Allah be upon him, has told us and warned us about in these *hadiths*. What the Messenger of Allah, may the peace and blessings of Allah be upon him, most feared for his community was that this world would shower itself liberally upon them. He also feared, may the peace and blessings of Allah be upon him, that Allah would open the flower of the *Dunya* to the Muslims and that its beauty would dazzle them. As he said, peace and blessings be upon him, "Truly I am more afraid for you of the trial of joys and pleasures than I am of the trial of difficulties and hardship."

What should we make of this uninterrupted stream of warnings about the flower of the life of this world? The answer is that faith is an expression of upward movement towards the height and sublimity of what is with Allah, may He be exalted, and man is not able to combine at the same time an aspiration towards a thing with its opposite. He can only devote himself to one of them. If someone aspires to the *Dunya* and devotes himself to it, he necessarily becomes heedless and negligent in the affairs of the *Akhira*. If, however, he devotes himself to the *Akhira*, he then becomes heedless of his attachment to the *Dunya* to such an extent that if the *Dunya* does accumulate for him he subjects his wealth to his more sublime project so that he may achieve the aim and purpose of the Next World.

> "When We desire to destroy a city, We send a command to the affluent in it and they become wantonly deviant in it and the Word is realised against it and We annihilate it completely." (17:16)

> "There is no city We will not destroy before the Day of Resurrection, or punish with a terrible punishment. That is inscribed in the Book." (17:58)

The affluent of any nation represent the class of the important and leisurely who possess wealth and have servants. They live a life of ease, of repose and mastery; but inevitably, as a result, they become soft and flabby, they become lethargic and they descend into corruption and madness. They belittle human and social values and denigrate sacred things and miracles. They become involved in dissent and forbidden things. If there is no one to restrain them, they will work corruption on the earth and cause immoral behaviour to spread throughout society.

When this happens among the Muslims the greater nation of Islam begins to disintegrate under the influence of spineless behaviour. It loses its vitality and the very elements which give it strength and vigour. It loses the very reasons for its continued existence, and then it perishes and its page in history is closed.

The above mentioned *ayats* show how Allah acts in such situations. If Allah has decreed that a town should be destroyed because it is acting in such a way as to bring down upon itelf this disaster and the people of affluence and extravagance are multiplying and no one is stopping or restraining them, then Allah will overpower this class of affluent persons by causing them to become corrupt and they will perish at their own hands. They will become weak and flabby and the *Sunna* of Allah will then be realised against them. They will be struck by disaster and perish.

The town itself is responsible for what happens because it does not put a stop to the power and authority of the affluent. The very existence of those who live in ease and extravagance means the whole town inevitably succumbs to their influence and their existence is the reason why Allah allows them to take control and bring about corruption. Were they to be put in their place and not allowed to dominate, the town would not merit destruction. If destruction was not decreed for a town, He would not allow people of corruption to establish their authority in it or allow them to lead it to perdition.

It is the Will of Allah that has established laws for the life of mankind which are immutable and established patterns of behaviour. Given that these fundamental laws of life have been laid out as natural limits, the destructive results which manifest in society will inevitably follow when those limits are breached. In this way the Will of Allah is carried out and His word comes true.

Allah does not order people to do what is corrupt or detrimental to human life for this is an abomination, and Allah would never order what is abominable. The existence of the affluent who lead a life of extravagance and luxury itself proves that the internal structure of a nation has broken down, that it is in the process of disintegrating and that the decree of Allah will inevitably strike its people with a punishment which fits their crime. So that is the punishment which people expose themselves to when they contravene the *Sunna* of Allah, when they permit the affluent to flourish and carry on their lives of luxury and extravagance.

The Will of Allah, however, is not unduly coercive, nor is it arbitrary or disconnected from the whole of the human process. The ultimate punishment of a people is the inevitable and direct result of their own actions. It is in this sense that the Divine Command is inescapable. In effect the whole of the *Sunna* of Allah is based around man's actions. Allah's command is not that man become corrupt: His command is the natural and inevitable outcome of the existence of the affluent and extravagant; what He decrees is a direct result of man's corruption.[1]

> Ad-Dinawari narrates from al-Hasan that Salman al-Farsi came to Abu Bakr as-Siddiq, may Allah be pleased with both of them, at the time of the illness from which he died and said, "Advise me, O Khalifa of the Messenger of Allah!" To which Abu Bakr replied, "Surely Allah will open up the *Dunya* for you, but let none of you take from it more than what is sufficient for his needs."

> Abu Nu'aym tells us in *Hilyat al-Awliya'* that 'Abd ar-Rahman ibn 'Awf, may Allah be pleased with him, said, "I went into where Abu Bakr was, may Allah be pleased with him, during the illness from which he died. I greeted him and then he said, "I see the *Dunya* approaching. When it stands before you and is moving towards you, you will take curtains of silk and cushions of brocade but you will be hurt by your soft upholstery as if you had sat on a

---

1. See Sayyid Qutb, *In the Shade of the Quran*, vol. 4, p. 2207.

thorn. By Allah, if one of you were to come forward and have his head cut off without it even being for a capital crime, it would be better for him than swimming in the sea of the *Dunya*."[1]

This world is only there so that we may take from it enough our needs. This is clear from Abu Bakr's words "…if one of you were to come forward and have his head cut off without it even being for a *hadd* punishment, it would be better for him than swimming in the sea of the *Dunya*." This is part of the law, the *fiqh* of Islam. Abu Bakr's position is a central teaching of Islam in that it exhorts people to beware of anything which might cause harm in the Next World for the Muslims.

> It is narrated that one of the Companions of the Prophet, may the peace and blessings of Allah be upon him, had a dream. The Prophet sent for him, and when he came he recounted the dream to the Prophet. This man happened to have a large stomach, and pushing his finger into his stomach the Prophet said, "If this were somewhere else it would be better for you." This is narrated by at-Tabarani. According to the narration of Ahmad it was the Prophet who had a dream about the man.

> Malik narrates from Yahya ibn Sa'id that 'Umar ibn al-Khattab, may Allah be pleased with him, caught up with Jabir ibn 'Abdullah, may Allah be pleased with him, when he was carrying some meat. 'Umar said: "Do none of you wish to tighten your belts around your stomachs for the sake of a neighbour or a cousin? How you have neglected the *ayat*: *'You dissipated your good things in your worldly life and enjoyed yourself in it!'* (46:19)"

Overeating and indigestion are dangerous. This danger does not only affect a person's health: there is also a risk that his capacity to think properly will be affected, and that it will endanger the well-being of his heart and weaken his certainty about Allah. What are the thoughts of the person who indulges in over-eating? What are

---

1. Meaning "so fine and delicate have you become in your life of ease."

the values he holds to? Such a person's interest and concern will not extend beyond his stomach and his gluttony. He will not be able to think about human values or the fundamentals of the *deen*. The Next World will not be the focus of his vision but rather his sight will be fixed on what will fill his stomach.

If he does have any picture of the Next World it will only be in accordance with his greed and voracious appetite. His state will be the same as the owner of the two gardens in *Surat al-Kahf* mentioned previously. His ego and envious greed take on such proportions that he imagines that the Next World will be the same for him as this world, which seems so subservient and obedient to him despite his pride and self-deceit. *"But if I should be sent back to my Lord, I will definitely get something better in return."* (18:36)

The believer's relationship to the world, on the other hand, is a relationship which is decreed and dictated by faith. It is limited and contained by the truths and realities of the Next World. He does not avail himself of anything from this world unless it fortifies him for the Next World.

'Umar ibn al-Khattab is obviously someone who reflected upon and truly understood his *deen*, someone who pondered the *ayats* of the Generous Qur'an. He was aware of the *ayat* which condemns those who will suffer torment and decribes their utter loss on the Day of Resurrection. 'Umar demands of us that we tighten our belts – for the sake of our brothers and our families. He demands that we understand how they feel and that we do not become distracted by our stomachs from the honour and glory of the Next World.

Fear and apprehension about the approach of the *dunya* and its beauty

> Ibn Mas'ud narrates that the Messenger of Allah, may the peace and blessings of Allah be upon him, declared: "The Hour is approaching, but for them it only increases in distance."[1]

1. Al-Haythami said that it is narrated by at-Tabarani whose narraters are sound; there is also has another narration with al-Bazzar.

This *hadith* points to an important truth and a strange condition in man. Thousands of years have elapsed since the time of the first Divine Revelation – that is, since the creation of Adam, though Allah knows best. There is no doubt that the passing of years means that the Last Day has been coming closer. We have read how fearful of the Last Day the first believers were. It is therefore logical to suppose that later generations would be more fearful than those who preceded them because they are closer to the Last Day. In fact one finds the exact opposite: the closer people are to the Last Day, the more reassured they appear to be, as if they had nothing to fear and were in complete safety.

Love of the *Dunya* has clouded their hearts. Their eyes have become blinded by the outward manifestations of affluence and extravagance. They have become beguiled by other people's attachment to the beauty and finery of such manifestations. As a result the Next World has become far removed from their consciousness and the clamour of the Last Day has receded in intensity in their ears. Remembrance of death has become burdensome for their hearts and so they have become blind and dumb. They have distanced themselves from the Next World by their reliance on the *dunya* and by their seeking permanent shelter in it. We ask Allah, may He be exalted, that we may be spared such a fate.

Al-Bazzar narrated the following from Zayd ibn Arqam, may Allah be pleased with him: "We were with Abu Bakr, may Allah be pleased with him, when he requested something to drink. He was brought water and honey. When it was placed in his hand, he wept and he continued until we thought there was something wrong with him. We did not question him then but when he had stopped, we said: "O Khalifa of the Messenger of Allah, may the peace and blessings of Allah be upon him, what caused you to weep like that?" He replied, "Once when I was with the Messenger of Allah, may the peace and blessings of Allah be upon him, I saw him pushing something away although I could not see anything. So I asked: 'Messenger of Allah, what is it that I see you pushing away but that I cannot see?' He replied: 'It is the *Dunya* which is reaching out to

me, so I told it: "Get back to yourself away from me."
Then it said to me, "You have not been caught by me.'"
Abu Bakr continued, 'That troubled me greatly and I
feared that I had contradicted the orders of the Messenger
of Allah, may the peace and blessings of Allah be upon
him, and that the *Dunya* had caught me.'"

The *Dunya* reached out to the Messenger of Allah, may the
peace and blessings of Allah be upon him, and offered itself to
him. But what is the *Dunya* if not a mere fleeting manifestation
and illusion? Is not the Prophet, may the peace and blessings of
Allah be upon him, the doctor who specialises in treating the
symptoms of the disease and in working to eradicate them from
the selves of men? Thus it is that he tells the *Dunya* to go back to
itself and keep its distance from him. It is as if the Messenger of
Allah, may the peace and blessings of Allah be upon him, is
speaking to the generations to come and saying: "I am calling you
to the Garden and warning against the deceit of the *Dunya,* so do
not exchange what is lasting for what is perishing, what is true for
what is delusion."

The Prophet pushed the *Dunya* away from himself, aware that
he was able and strong enough to overcome it, and it in turn recognised this and said to the Prophet: "You have not been caught by
me." Abu Bakr remembered this scene when he was brought water
and honey and feared that he had acted in opposition to the command of the Messenger of Allah, may the peace and blessings of
Allah be upon him, and the *Dunya* had got hold of him. What we
learn from this *hadith* is that to oppose the orders of the Mes-senger of Allah is dangerous and causes the believer to become heedless of the Next World and attached to this world.

Al-Bayhaqi narrates that al-Mansur ibn al-Makhrama
said, may Allah be pleased with him: "The booty of al-
Qadisiyya was brought to 'Umar ibn al-Khattab, may
Allah be pleased with him, and as he set about examining
it and looking at it he wept. With him was 'Abd ar-
Rahman ibn 'Awf, may Allah be pleased with him, who
said to him: "Commander of the Believers, this is a day of

celebration, this is a day of happiness." 'Umar replied, "Yes, but such things are never given to a people without them also inheriting emnity and hate."

Al-Hasan narrates that the crown jewels of Chosroes were brought and placed before 'Umar ibn al-Khattab, may Allah be pleased with him, and amongst the people present was Suraqa ibn Malik ibn Ju'sham, may Allah be pleased with him. 'Umar said, "Put the bracelets and arm rings of Chosroes on him (Suraqa)." He put them on his arm and they reached his shoulders. When 'Umar saw them on Suraqa's arms he said, "Praise belongs to Allah that the armbands of Chosroes are on the arm of Suraqa ibn Malik Ju'sham, a Bedouin Arab from the Banu Mudlij." Then he said: "O Allah, I know that Your Messenger, may the peace and blessings of Allah be upon him, loved to receive wealth and then spend it in Your Cause and on Your slaves, but You kept it back from him out of solicitude for him by Your choice." Then he said: "O Allah, I knew that Abu Bakr, may Allah be pleased with him used to like to receive wealth and spend it in Your way and on Your slaves, but You kept it back from him out of solicitude for him by Your choice. O Allah, I seek refuge in You lest it be a stratagem from you concerning 'Umar." Then he recited: *"Do they imagine that, in the wealth and children We extend to them, We are hastening to them with good things? No indeed, but they are not aware!"* (23:55-56)

'Umar said: "I heard the Messenger of Allah say, may the peace and blessings of Allah be upon him: *'Dunya* is not opened up for any people without Allah, may He be glorified, causing emnity and hate to come between them until the Day of Resurrection; and I am afraid on account of this.'"

When we read this we should reflect upon 'Umar ibn al-Khattab's weeping, may Allah be pleased with him, on a day which should have been a day of celebration and joy. We do not

144

find that the Commander of the Believers is perplexed or astonished when there is wealth before him or that he is transfixed by the flower and beauty of the life of this world. Rather he quickly calls to mind the influence of this wealth on the relations between people and he remembers how the Prophet, may the peace and blessings of Allah be upon him, had warned that wealth is one of the causes of enmity and hatred between people. This warning is not forgotten by 'Umar ibn al-Khattab because he sees matters with an insight based on faith and belief. How insignificant wealth is for him, viewed as it is through this insight based on faith!

Wealth is one of the reasons for enmity and hatred but it is also a cause of greed and egoistical desires. It is a door to destruction and discord, so reflect on 'Umar's prayer to his Lord when he has the wealth of Chosroes before him. 'Umar, may Allah be pleased with him, fears that the victory and the subsequent taking of booty will be a cause of destruction or a test. Allah, may He be exalted, says: *"We will lead them, step by step, into destruction from where they do not know."* (7:182) And 'Umar recollects Allah's words: *"Do they imagine that, in the wealth and children We extend to them, We are hastening to them with good things? No indeed, but they are not aware!"* (23:55-56) His understanding shows that he is truly aware, aware of the position of the believer in life with respect to its pleasures.

Abu Wa'il Shaqiq ibn Salama said: "We went in to where Khabbab ibn al-Aratt was during his illness and he said: 'There is eighty thousand dirhams in this casket. I have not locked them up or prevented them being given to beggars." Then he wept and we said, 'Why are you weeping?' He replied, 'I am weeping because my companions have taken the reward and the *Dunya* did not cause them to suffer any any deficit (in their reckoning) but we remain after them and we have not found a place for these (dirhams) other than the earth." Abu Nu'aym said that Abu Usama related from Idris that he said: "I would surely have preferred it to be such and such a thing," – and it was as if was saying "animal droppings" or some such thing.

145

This then was the reality of the *Dunya* in the eyes of Khabbab ibn al-Aratt, may Allah be pleased with him. He was envious of his companions who had taken the reward and had not suffered any deficit in their reckoning because of their possessions in the world and he wept in despair at having acquired great wealth which was only destined for the earth – meaning perhaps that he had acquired land or erected buildings.

Khabbab, one must remember, had earned his wealth in a permitted way and had not locked it up or prevented it from being given to those in need. But despite this he felt the burden of responsibility before Allah. What then did his wealth represent in his eyes? "I would surely have preferred it to be such and such a thing," – and it was as if he was saying "animal droppings" or some such thing. So it was of no worth at all in his eyes.

What then are we to think of those people who earn their wealth from forbidden sources or who on occasions mix the forbidden with the permitted and who do not fulfil the rights of Allah regarding what they earn? And these same people are the most intensely covetous of the wealth they have acquired. They put it in steel safes and secure them with further locks and bolts. What then will be their fate when they stand and face their responsibities before Allah, may He be exalted?

Abu 'Ubayda, Ibn Sa'd and Ibn Rahawayh report that Ibn 'Abbas, may Allah be pleased with him, said, "'Umar ibn al-Khattab, may Allah be pleased with him, called for me. When I came to him he had a leather bag in front of him full of gold. He said, 'Come and divide this among your people. Allah knows best why He kept this back from His Prophet, may the peace and blessings of Allah be upon him, and from Abu Bakr, and why I have been given it. Have I been given it for good or for evil?' Then he wept and said: 'No, by the One Who has my self in His hands, He did not keep it back it from His Prophet and from Abu Bakr out of ill will towards them both – and He gave it to 'Umar out of good will towards him.'"

It is narrated in al-Bukhari that Khabbab said, "We made *Hijra* with the Prophet, may the peace and blessings of

146

Allah be upon him, seeking the Face of Allah, and our reward was incumbent upon Allah. One of those who passed on and who did not consume any of their reward was Mus'ab ibn 'Umayr, may Allah be pleased with him. He was killed at the battle of Uhud and left nothing but a striped cloth. When we covered his head with it his legs stuck out and when we covered his legs his head stuck out. Then the Prophet, may the peace and blessings of Allah be upon him, said, 'Cover his head with it and place matting over his legs. There are those among us whose fruit ripen and they will pick them.'"

Much wealth and booty was held back from the Messenger of Allah, may the peace and blessings of Allah be upon him and from Abu Bakr, may Allah be pleased with him but the doors (of abundance) were opened wide for 'Umar, may Allah be pleased with him. Allah did not keep this wealth from his two predecessors out of any ill will towards either of them, and 'Umar was only given it out of good will towards him. His nervousness about it is one of the signs of his scrupulousness, may Allah be pleased with him. As we have already mentioned above, that was what he taught others in the Community. 'Umar himself was a brilliant star amongst other the other stars who were the Companions of the Messenger of Allah, may Allah bless him and grant him peace, and of whom he said, "Whichever of them you follow you will be guided." May Allah be pleased with all of them. 'Umar himself was all generosity, justice and asceticsim.

Al-Bukhari narrates from 'Uqba ibn 'Amir, may Allah be pleased with him, that the Messenger of Allah may the peace and blessings of Allah be upon him, passed by the dead Muslim warriors of Uhud as if he were taking his farewell of the living and the dead. He then ascended the *minbar* and said, "I am the one who will go ahead of you, and I shall be a witness over you and certainly your appointed place is the Basin (of the Garden) which I can see from where I am standing. I do not fear that you will associate others with Allah. What I do fear for you is this

world and that you will vie with each other for it." 'Uqba
said, "That was the last time I saw the Messenger of Allah,
may the peace and blessings of Allah be upon him."

It is recorded in al-Bukhari – in the section on slaves –
from 'Uqba ibn 'Amir that the Prophet, may the peace and
blessings of Allah be upon him, went out one day and
prayed over the Muslims who had been killed at Uhud.
After mentioning them, he declared: "By Allah, surely I
am looking even now at my Basin (in the Garden) and I
have been given the keys of the treasures of the earth" – or
(in another version) "the keys of the earth – and truly, by
Allah, I do not fear that you will associate others with
Allah after I have gone but I fear that you will vie with
each other over this (world)."

The two Shaykhs (al-Bukhari and Muslim) narrate from
'Amr ibn 'Awf al-Ansari, may Allah be pleased with him
that the Messenger of Allah, may the peace and blessings
of Allah be upon him, sent Abu 'Ubayda ibn al-Jarrah,
may Allah be pleased with him, to Bahrain to collect its
jizya. He arrived with much wealth from Bahrain and the
Ansar heard of his arrival. They came to the dawn prayer
with the Messenger of Allah. When the Messenger of
Allah, may the peace and blessings of Allah be upon him,
had prayed, he started to leave and they approached him.
The Messenger of Allah smiled when he saw them and
said, "I suppose that you have heard that Abu 'Ubayda has
brought something from Bahrain?" They replied, "Yes,
Messenger of Allah!" He said, "Rejoice and look forward
to what will make you happy, for by Allah, I do not fear
poverty for you but I fear that the *Dunya* will extend itself
liberally before you – as it extended itself liberally to those
before you – and you will vie with each other for it as they
vied with each other for it and it will destroy you as it
destroyed them."

It is worth repeating this *hadith* because of its relevance to this
section. The Messenger of Allah, may the peace and blessings of

Allah be upon him, knew the pleasures of this world and the self-delusion and the attachment to the heart which are occasioned by them. Such an attachment gives rise to covetousness and greed and this in turn engenders heavy reliance on the lower self, with the corresponding effect on behaviour which such reliance induces. It is this which causes people to fight and vie with one another. The more people believe in themselves the more removed they become from the realities of true belief and faith and the closer comes their inevitable destruction.

An increase in the goods of the *Dunya* is a trial and its pleasures are an irresistible attraction. Then people drown in the delights of this life and pleasure overwhelms them and they become completely identified with their own lower selves. The result is that the enjoining of good and the forbidding of evil are forgotten; an atmosphere of vainglory and greed for gathering the stuff of this world prevails; desires and lust overwhelm man and his appetites and emotions dominate his being; his intellect diminishes and apathy and indifference reign. The only thinking he does is to try and pacify his conscience, and he is only excited by those things which intensify those aspects of delight and pleasure in his life.

The intellect thus becomes subjected to the whims and caprices of the lower self. People's behaviour becomes ugly and deformed. The person who outstrips the others in chasing after sensual pleasures and who is dominated by lusts and desires becomes an example for others, the highest model to be followed. People of this kind will take from the *deen* whatever justifies their desires and whatever will endear them to the world and the laws they invent serve only to justify such desires, to fulfil the desires they want to gratify.

These are some of the implications of this *hadith* of the Messenger of Allah, which warns us of the dangers of the *Dunya*, especially when it becomes freely available to people. Such temptations and trials can destroy whole generations – even nations. They can shake the very foundations of society as they open the door to self-delusion and deceit. Such a situation is in some ways even more dangerous than associating others with Allah (*shirk*) –

149

may Allah protect us from such a thing – because the state of the person guilty of association is evident whereas that of the person who is attached to the *Dunya* may not be.

The pattern of behaviour of the former is manifestly doomed to destruction, whereas that of the latter can never be known for certain and only Allah knows who is protected from such trials and temptations. The Prophet, may the peace and blessings of Allah be upon him, compared an abundance of *Dunya* and people's vying each other for it with the association of others with Allah, and did so as a warning against such abundance and excess and as a reminder of its danger.

> 'Abdullah ibn 'Umar narrates that the Messenger of Allah, may the peace and blessings of Allah be upon him, declared, "Successful is he who submits and becomes a Muslim, has sufficient provision, and is made content by Allah."[1]

> Fadala ibn 'Ubayd says that he heard the Messenger of Allah say, may the peace and blessings of Allah be upon him: "Good it is for those who are guided to Islam, whose daily provision is sufficient, and who are contented."[2]

This world is what distracts us from the Next World. The more a person has of the *Dunya*, the further his worship becomes from Allah, may He be exalted. The Messenger, may the peace and blessings of Allah be upon him, has provided in himself a model for us to follow. He was offered riches but he refused them and preferred to live life in all its different states, sometimes eating his fill and sometimes going hungry, in order to be continually aware of His Lord. This is the true state of the human being who does exist by his own essence but only by the generosity of his Lord. So the believer is poor, dependent on Allah, his heart attached to his Sustainer.

The three elements which ensure success are Islam, sufficiency of provision, meaning what is necessary to fulfil one's basic needs, and contentment with what one has.

---

1. According to at-Tirmidhi says this is a sound *hadith*.
2. According to at-Tirmidhi says that this is a good and sound *hadith*.

Abu Dharr narrates that the Prophet, may the peace and blessings of Allah be upon him, said, "Detachment in the *Dunya* means that you should not feel more sure of what is in your hands now than of what is still in the hands of Allah, and that you should prefer the reward for an affliction – should it strike you – to remain with you."[1]

This absolute trust in Allah – being more certain of what is still with Allah than what is already in your own hands – and preferring the reward for an affliction – are the two basic elements which form the character of a person who is characterised by detachment from the world. Detachment, then, is not love of poverty and abandoning the good things of life, but rather an elevated faith and belief and a trust in Allah, may He be exalted, and a desire for His reward.

The excellence of being content with what Allah gives

'Abdu'l-A'la ibn ash-Shukhayr said, "One of the Banu Salim told me, and I cannot but think that he saw the Messenger of Allah, may the peace and blessings of Allah be upon him, 'Surely Allah, may He be glorified, tests His slave by what He gives him. Whoever is content with what Allah, may He be exalted, has apportioned him, Allah will bless him in it and will increase his portion; but whoever is not content will not be blessed in what he has.'"[2]

Allah, may He be exalted, tests His slave by what He gives him, as He says: *"As for man, when his Lord puts him to the test by honouring him and blessing him, he says, 'My Lord has honoured me.' But then when He puts him to the test by restricting his provision, he says, 'My Lord has humiliated me.'"* (99:15-18) If someone is content with what Allah, may He be exalted, has

---

1. According to at-Tirmidhi this is a *gharib hadith* and that its chain of narration contains 'Amr ibn Waqid who is not recognised as a transmitter of *hadith*.

2. Narrated by Ahmad in his *Musnad*.

apportioned him, then his portion also contains *baraka* – blessing and increase – and so what was a small portion becomes in effect a large portion and what was difficult becomes easy. Allah then puts a feeling of independence and richness in his heart. But as for those who are not content with what Allah has apportioned them and are angry with what He, may He be praised, gives them, Allah will strip any blessing from their provision, will increase their greed and will multiply their anxieties and worries.

> Anas ibn Malik narrates that the Prophet said, may the peace and blessings of Allah be upon him: "Whoever awakes despondent at the world also awakes angry at his Lord, may He be exalted, and whoever awakes complaining of an affliction which has befallen him is complaining of Allah, may He be exalted. Whoever humbles himself to a rich person, in order to obtain something of what he has, makes Allah angry, may He be exalted, and whoever is given the Qur'an and then enters the Fire, Allah will remove him from it."[1]

The *Dunya* is of scant worth. We have read what the Messenger of Allah has said of it, "This world is cursed ... and what is in it is cursed except for remembrance of Allah and whoever perseveres in it or the man of knowledge or the one acquiring knowledge." We have also read that Allah, may He be exalted, withholds the *Dunya* from His believing slave just as one of us might withhold water from a sick person in his care whom he loves. So why should there be any sadness on account of this world?

This *hadith* warns the believers not to become sad for the sake of the *Dunya,* for whoever awakes despondent on account of the *Dunya* is in fact awaking angry with his Lord. A believer does not become despondent because of something of this world he has missed out on, nor does he complain to his Lord. Believers do not leave each other in the lurch in order to obtain wealth from someone in authority, for they are desirous of what is with Allah, not of what is with people.

---

1. Al-Haythami says that at-Tabarani narrates this in *as-Saghir* and in the chain of narration is Wahb ibn Rashid al-Basri, a confirmed Companion.

'Abdullah ibn Mas'ud relates that the Messenger of Allah, may the peace and blessings of Allah be upon him, said, "Whoever is stricken by poverty and visits it upon other people, his poverty will not be alleviated; but whoever is stricken by poverty and submits it to Allah, Allah will be quick to send him provision in this world or the Next."[1]

The cries of people are intensifying, their state and circumstances are worsening, the springs of contentment are drying up. People are only to be seen complaining of their lack of fortune in life, lamenting what they find to be their straitened circumstances, bewailing those earlier days they passed in ease and prosperity.

The complaints of the rich despite their riches is a manifestation of a search, a dissatisfaction like that of a discontented child and the distress of poor people in their poverty. Wages are insufficient, the rising cost of living smothers people's potential so that they are always in difficulties and in a state of deprivation. All this is increasing at a time when the different political parties are establishing programmes which would cost a great amount of time and effort and money to implement but make little change. Governments promise their peoples a life of ease year after year but individuals end up with paltry amounts to live on and everyone needs more.

This *hadith* awakens in people a sense of faith and belief. Whenever one has a need or feels poverty-stricken, he should take his condition to the One Who created this need or poverty. He should stand with his need at the door of his Lord, Creator and Provider, for He alone is capable of fulfilling this need. If he takes his complaint to people, he is making a mistake. Why should anyone take their need to people who are themselves in need? Why do people ask of someone who is in reality incapable of helping them? If one takes his need to people, it will not be fulfilled but if he brings it before Allah, He will be quick to bring relief.

This *hadith* will do much to put the believer at ease regarding those who take pleasure in the unhappiness of others and delight in seeing disaster and affliction befall them. What could be better

1. At-Tirmidhi says that this is a good and sound *hadith* although *gharib*.

153

for these believers than to hand over their needs to their Lord in such times of affliction?

> Abu Hurayra narrates that the Messenger of Allah, may the peace and blessings of Allah be upon him, said: "Whoever becomes hungry or needy and then hides this from people and takes it to Allah, it is incumbent upon Allah to open up a year's lawful provision for him."[1]

If you conceal your need from people, you gain in stature and you become self-sufficient and independent. Your riches will derive from your seeking refuge with Allah, may He be exalted. He says, may He be exalted: *"If anyone desires to have might, might belongs altogether to Allah."* (35:10) And He also says: *"To Allah belongs might and to His Messenger and to the believers."* (63:8) This might comes to them by virtue of their sincere worship of Allah Almighty.

One of the qualities contributing to perfection in worship of Allah, may He be praised, is that of concealing one's need from people and instead bringing it before Allah, may He be exalted, for *"He possesses the treasure stores of the heavens and earth,"* (63:7) although most people do not realise it.

> Ibn 'Umar narrates that the Messenger of Allah said, may the peace and blessings of Allah be upon him: "A people are not patient in affliction for three days without Allah giving them provision."[2]

"Patience is the key to relief" from affliction and it is an indication of faith and certainty of belief. Indeed it represents half of faith and is also one of the means of coming close to Allah, may He be exalted. Complaining about one's state is a sign of lack of faith and absence of trust in the Divine Decree on the part of the believer. Patience is also the foundation of Islam, for it is a means

---

1. According to al-Haythami at-Tabarani narrated this in *as-Saghir* and *al-Awsat* and the chain of narration includes Isma'il ibn Raja al-Hisni who is regarded as weak by al-Daraqutni.

2. Al-Haythami says that this is narrated by Abu Ya'la, whose transmitters are trustworthy.

of salvation for the slave of Allah in the worst of situations. Patience is a kind of blessing for which the slave should be thankful when his situation becomes easier.

"We shall certainly test you with a certain amount of fear and hunger and loss of wealth and life and fruits. But give good news to the steadfast." (2:154)

These words from the Qur'an speak of another aspect of life, namely the inevitability of the believer being put to the test. There are various aspects to this testing which are mentioned here. The first is a certain amount of fear, meaning a slight amount. Despite this, however, one sees people in a permanent state of anxiety. What one may ask, would be our state of mind if Allah were to unleash a great amount of fear on to us? Then there is a certain amount of hunger, loss of wealth, loss of life and loss of fruits. And the good news in the end is for people with patience, the steadfast.

We can compare this with another *ayat*: *"You will be tested in your wealth and in your selves and you will hear many harmful words from those given the Book before you and from those who worship idols. But if you are steadfast and godfearing, that shows true resolve."* (3:186) As you can see, this *ayat* reveals other aspects of the testing. It refers to specific ways in which a person's self and his wealth may be tested and also how a person's beliefs may be put to the test. A believer, however, should be patient and steadfast, in the face of such trials, but that will only be possible for those who have acquired resolve.

So believers will be afflicted by a certain amount of fear, but they will be patient and things will turn out well in the end. They will also find reassurance with Allah. They will be tested in all the various ways mentioned, but the real disaster will strike when they come face to face with the difficulties and hardships caused by those who have already been given the Book and from those who associate other gods with Allah – that is, when they torment and attack them and ambush them. This type of persecution which is verbal will inevitably be directed at the root of the believers' faith.

They will have no qualms about attacking the Messenger of Allah, may the peace and blessings of Allah be upon him, or criticising the Qur'an, since they do not believe in either of them.

I am very much aware that the strength of unbelief has increased and there are all kinds of stratagems and conspiracies afoot against the Muslims. Attempts are being made to make them renounce their *deen*. The Muslim has two great weapons to defend himself against such attacks: patience and fear of God. With these two qualities resolution appears in a person. These two qualities are the basis of such resolve and constitute the real strength of the believer.

The World of Imagination and Semblance

Consider the nature of a mirror, an object with which every person, even every child, daily comes into contact. Many do not give it a second thought, so used are they to its presence – so much so that no one reflects on the reality of this object. It is a polished sheet of glass capable of transmitting a whole world to you. Your image is repeated again and again each time you look in a mirror, and this same mirror can effortlessly reflect fields stretching away into the distance.

Anyone looking into a mirror may see as much as he wants to see. You see fields before you in the mirror but in reality there are no fields. In the same way there may be a person reflected in the mirror but in reality there is no one there. Anything may appear to be there in front of you but in fact there is nothing. All one has to do is to cover up the mirror or break it for the image to disappear.

This is an exact metaphor of the *Dunya*. You see things in front of you, the number of reflected images is countless; then suddenly all of this can disappear. But it only disappears from your life, not from the life of anyone else; for you alone have broken the mirror. As for the others, they are able to see other images in their mirrors – until, that is, they break them and the images disappear. When the images disappear, reality manifests itself and the truth becomes clear to them – that it was only a mirror and that what held their attention was merely a thin space of air previously occupied by the mirror. Despite the illusion of space and distance the thickness of the glass only measured a few millimetres.

There is no power and no strength but by Allah! The lessons to be drawn are numerous. You are in front of the mirror but it is a false image, so do not be deceived by falsehood. You have to be careful not to regard it as reality. One of the lessons to be learnt is that the mirror does not normally break: in other words, the illusion is usually maintained. Another is that the mirror is well polished and things are clearly and brightly reflected in it. As time passes, however, that brilliance fades and the glass turns yellow. Things which appeared to shine in the reflection begin to dim. Mirrors, like all things, change in appearance. What was once beautiful and polished becomes faded and dull.

Look at your own self and essence and you will see wonders. When you were a child you found everything around you to be beautiful; you wanted to embrace life and you were full of desire for all manifestations of life. The mirror was still shiny and the images in it were bright and shiny. With the passing of time, however, as we advance in age, the mirror begins to dim and the images manifested fade and time weighs heavily on us. I am not saying that your connection to the mirror has lessened or that your desire for life has faded, but rather that the ties binding you to it are loosening and your sight is not as sharp as it was.

Man becomes so attached to the past that he is incapable of seeing the future. He looks with so much nostalgia at what happened earlier in his life that he finds the reality of his present life constricting. Food no longer tastes as appetizing as it used to in his childhood or in his youth. Places no longer hold the same allure as they did when he was young. His greed and covetousness increase while his strength and capacity decrease. His love of the *Dunya* grows while his capacity for enjoying it diminishes. Read the words of the Messenger of Allah, may the peace and blessings of Allah be upon him: "Seize hold of five things before five others: your youth before your old age; your health before your illness; your leisure before your occupation; your independence and riches before your poverty; and your life before your death." We ask Allah that He spare us and grant us health and strength.

157

Conclusion

In conclusion I feel that it is incumbent upon me to dwell for a moment with you upon the words of Imam 'Ali, may Allah be pleased with him and may Allah ennoble his face: "One aspect of the insignificance of this world in the sight of Allah is that only in it can acts of disobedience be committed and that only by leaving it can one attain what is with Him." Allah does not permit acts of disobedience except on the earth.

When Iblis refused to prostrate before Adam and disobeyed his Lord, his Lord said to him: *"Descend from Heaven. It is not for you to be arrogant in it. So get out!"* (7:12) When Adam ate from the tree under the influence of Iblis's guile his Lord commanded him to leave the Garden. The inhabitants of the Fire will be obedient and humble once they are in it and will not rebel even though they will cry out and call in anguish from their state of loss and perdition. They are clearly ready to obey, as they will say: *"Our Lord, we have seen and we have heard, so send us back again and we will act rightly."* (32:12)

We will not obtain the reward that is with Allah, however, unless we abandon this world. Anyone who desires the Next World must diminish his ties with this world. As the Messenger of Allah said, may the peace and blessings of Allah be upon him, in a *hadith* we looked at earlier: "Anyone who loves his *Dunya* will harm his *Akhira* and anyone who loves his *Akhira* will harm his *Dunya*."

We ask Allah for pardon and health and strength and we ask Him to save us from the Fire.

And praise belongs to the Lord of the Worlds.

Glossary

Adha: the Festival of Sacrifice at the end of the *hajj*.

Akhira: the Hereafter, the Next World which is everlasting. It is the opposite of *Dunya*.

awliya' : plural of *wali*, someone who is a 'friend' of Allah.

ayat: a verse of the Qur'an

Bayt al-Mal: The public treasury of the Muslims.

deen: the life-transaction, lit. the debt between two parties, in this usage between the Creator and created.

Dunya: this lower world in the sense of temporal and ephemeral things.

fiqh: the science of the application of the *Shari'a*. A practitioner or expert in *fiqh* is called a *faqih*.

fitra: the first nature, the natural, primal condition of mankind in harmony with nature.

gharib: 'scarce, strange'; in the science of *Hadith*, it designates a tradition which has a single transmitter at some stage of the *isnad*, or chain of transmission.

hadd: Allah's boundary limits which define the lawful and unlawful. The *hadd* punishments are specific fixed penalties laid down by Allah for specified crimes.

hadith: authenticated reported speech of the Prophet.

halal: permitted by the *Shari'a*.

haram: forbidden by the *Shari'a*.

Hijra: emigration for the Cause of Allah, especially designating the emigration of the Prophet from Makka to Madina.

hudud: plural of *hadd*.

Iblis: Shaytan or the Devil.

ihsan: the state of being absolutely sincere to Allah.

iman: belief, acceptance, faith.

jihad: struggle, particularly fighting in the Cause of Allah to establish and defend Islam.

jizya: a tax imposed on non-Muslims under the protection of Muslim rule.

Mi'raj: the Night Journey of the Prophet from Jerusalem to heaven.

minbar: steps on which the Imam stands to deliver the *khutba* or sermon at the Friday communal prayer.

sadaqa: giving for the sake of Allah, a charitable gift without any ulterior motive.

salihun: the plural of *salih*, a spiritually developed person who acts righteously.

Shari'a: The legal modality of a people based on the revelation received or followed by their Prophet. The final *Shari'a* is that of Islam.

Shaytan: a devil, particularly Iblis.

shirk: the unforgivable wrong action of worshipping something or someone other than Allah or associating something or someone as a partner with Him.

Sunna: the customary practice of a person or group of people. It has come to refer almost exclusively to the practice of the Messenger of Allah.

sura: chapter of the Qur'an.

tafsir: commentary or explanation of the meanings of the ayats of the Noble Qur'an.

ta'ala: "Exalted is He," an Arabic expression frequently used to honour Allah.

taqwa: awe or fear of Allah, which inspires a person to guard against doing wrong and eager for actions which please Him.

umma: the Community of Muslims as ideally one distinct and integrated body.

zakat: a wealth tax, one of the five Pillars of Islam.